The *Woman* I'm Becoming

TANYA STOKES

Copyright © 2025 by Tanya Stokes

All rights reserved. No part of this publication may be reproduced, distributed, or transmitted in any form or by any means, including photocopying, recording, or other electronic or mechanical methods, without the prior written permission of the publisher, except in the case of brief quotations embodied in critical reviews and certain other noncommercial uses permitted by copyright law. For permission requests, write to the publisher, addressed "Attention: Permissions Coordinator," at the email address below.

ISBN: 978-1-959370-27-7, Hardback
Edited by: Tanya Stokes
Book Production: Compassionate Designs Publishing
Book Design: Compassionate Designs, Tanya Stokes
Printed by Amazon in the United States of America.
Email: CDP.Publishing@gmail.com
Published in USA

Dedication

To the ones who came before me—
Whose strength hums in my veins like a steady drumbeat,
Carrying wisdom, courage, and prayers I never heard aloud,
But felt in every step I took forward.

To the women who raised me—
In silence, in grit, in grace.
You taught me that survival is sacred,
That rising isn't always loud—sometimes, it's just choosing to breathe again.

To Tiernan my son —
Your name is woven into every sentence,
Every ache, every triumph, every whispered prayer for strength.
You are my anchor and my wings.
You showed me that love doesn't vanish—it expands.
It echoes. It births purpose.
This book is as much yours as it is mine.

To Kendra "K-LA" Anderson—
My sister in spirit, my laughter in the dark, my mirror and my safe space. Over 30 years of friendship, of finishing each other's sentences, of surviving life's twists with music, mischief, and moments only we could understand.
Your absence is loud, but your presence is louder.
You live in my boldness. You live in these pages.

You believed in me when I didn't. You held me together when I was unraveling.
This book carries your fingerprints—
Every word a tribute, every chapter a piece of our forever.

To the woman holding this book—
This is for every time you felt invisible.
For every moment you hid your power.
For the nights you cried quietly, and the mornings you rose anyway.
You are seen. You are worthy. You are not alone.

May these pages find you exactly where you are
And gently pull you toward where you're meant to go.

This is more than a book—
It is my heartbeat in print.
A love letter.
A legacy.
A call to rise.

For you.
For me.
For K-LA.
For the woman we're still becoming.

— Tanya

Acknowledgments

To God—my anchor, my guide, and my strength. Thank you for never leaving me, even in the shadows.

To the woman I'm still becoming—thank you for not giving up on me.

With all my heart,

Tanya

Contents

Part I. Foundation & Identity

Chapter 1: The Woman I'm Becoming 3

Chapter 2: Mental and Spiritual Growth:
Nurturing Your Inner Power 15
The Power of Mindset 17
Spiritual Growth: Going Deeper
Than the Surface 18
Practices That Fuel Inner Power 19
Rewriting the Narrative 20
A Personal Becoming Moment 21

Chapter 3: Unlearning the Lies 27
The Lies We Tell Ourselves (And
Where They Came From) 29
The Power of Unlearning 30
A Personal Becoming Moment 30
How to Start Unlearning 31
Let's Talk About Cultural Lies 32
The Emotional Weight of Unlearning 33

Chapter 4: Take the Time to Get to Know Yourself 39
Why Self-Knowledge Matters 40
Who Am I, Really? 41
A Personal Becoming Moment 42

	Simple Ways to Get to Know Yourself..........43
Chapter 5:	The Power of Vulnerability...........................49
	Vulnerability is a Strength, not a Symptom 50
	Why We Hide (And How It Hurts Us) 51
	A Personal Becoming Moment 51
	How We Confuse Vulnerability with Weakness..53
	Practicing Vulnerability Without Losing Yourself...53
	When Vulnerability Becomes a Superpower 54
	Everyday Moments to Be Vulnerable...........55

Part II. *Healing & Self-Worth*

Chapter 6:	Love Deprived...63
	The Emotional Dive......................................64
	The Courage to Name It 64
	A Personal Becoming Moment 65
	Passionate Truth 67
Chapter 7:	Learning to Love Yourself First 73
	The Lies We've Been Told.............................74
	What Loving Yourself Looks Like................75
	A Personal Becoming Moment 75
	Simple Ways to Practice Self-Love Daily.......77
Chapter 8:	Learning to Say "No" 83
	Why Saying No Is So Hard 85
	The Power Behind the No............................85
	Say No with Confidence and Compassion ...86

	A Tool for Practicing Your No: The Boundary Filter 86
	A Personal Moment of Choosing Me 87
Chapter 9:	Be Selfish About Your Time..........................93
	Time as a Reflection of Values 94
	The Guilt Trap 95
	Practical Boundaries to Reclaim Your Time 95
	A Personal Becoming Moment: Boundary Breakthrough 96
Chapter 10:	Pour Into Yourself Before You Pour into Others..103
	The Burnout Cycle....................................105
	Reclaiming the Word 'Selfish'.....................105
	A Personal Becoming Moment: Refill........106
Chapter 11:	Communication Isn't a Cuss Word-*K-LA*...113
	Why We Stay Silent...................................114
	A Personal Becoming Moment: Speak Up..115
	Healthy Communication Looks Like: 116
	How to Practice Brave Communication 117
Chapter 12:	Distraction: How to Avoid It and Stay Focused..123
	The Real Cost of Distraction......................124
	Common Distractions and How to Handle Them...125
	My Personal Wake-Up Call 126
	A Personal Becoming Moment: When I Faced My Own Noise....................127
	Reclaiming Your Focus...............................128

Chapter 13: Protecting Your Peace 133
        Why Peace Feels So Hard to Maintain........134
        Signs Your Peace Is Under Attack 135
        A Personal Becoming Moment:
        When I Said No to Chaos 136
        Protecting Your Peace in Real Life 137
        Peace vs. Performance.................................137
        What Protecting Peace Really Means..........138
        Protecting Peace at Home...........................138
        Protecting Peace in Relationships 139

Chapter 14: Unlearning Desperation 145
        Calling It What It Is.....................................146
        A Personal Becoming Moment:
        Breakthrough 147
        The Process of Unlearning...........................148
        The Courage to Let Go 148

Part III. Alignment & Embodiment

Chapter 15: Redefining Success 155
        Why We Need a New Definition 156
        The Sneaky Pressure to Perform 157
        A Personal Shift..157
        What Does Success Mean to YOU?............158
        Red Flags You're Living Someone
        Else's Version of Success...............................159
        Redefining Success Practically.....................159
        When Slowing Down IS Success 160
        The Inner Success Inventory 160

Chapter 16: Achieving the Goals, Dreams, and
        Aspirations You Desire 167
        Getting Clear on What You Really Want....169

  Facing the Fear 169
  Making a Plan and Taking Action 170
  A Personal Becoming Moment: 171

Chapter 17: Come Out of the Shadows and Into
  the Light 177
  Why We Hide 179
  Light Doesn't Mean Perfect 179
  The Moment I Stepped Into the Light 180
  A Personal Becoming Moment 180
  The Cost of Dimming 182
  Stepping Boldly Into the Light 182

Chapter 18: Be That Before You Expect It-K-LA 187
  You Can't Call in What You Keep
  Canceling Out 189
  A Personal Becoming Moment: The
  Mirror Moment 190

Chapter 19: Becoming Her—In Action 195
  Becoming Her Is a Daily Decision 196
  Your Becoming Checklist 197
  A Personal Becoming Moment 197
  Becoming Her Is Not Linear 198
  Your Daily Becoming Practice 199
  Habits That Support Her 199

Part IV. *Legacy & Reflection*

Chapter 20: My Life Journey and the Lessons I've
  Learned 207
  Lesson 1: You can break and still bloom. 208
  Lesson 2: Grief is not a weakness. It's
  a form of love. 209

Lesson 3: Forgiveness is freedom. 209
Lesson 4: God's timing > my timeline. 209
Lesson 5: I am enough—even when
I'm evolving...210

Part I

FOUNDATION & IDENTITY

Chapter 1
The Woman I'm Becoming

Let's be clear: this is no ordinary book.

If you're looking for a polished, perfect guide with ten flawless steps to becoming the ideal woman—put this book down, sis. This ain't it.

This book has stretch marks. It's got laugh lines and soul scars. It's the book that wears cozy socks, sips tea (or wine, depending on the day), and talks to you like your honest, no-filter best friend. The one who's going to tell you when you're glowing and also when you're slipping.

We're about to laugh, cry, reflect, and probably shout "yesss!" at least once or twice. So take a breath, unclench your jaw, and let your shoulders relax. You're in safe, sacred space now.

Let's begin.

The Woman I'm Becoming

She's not who she used to be—
and she's not quite who she's going to be.
But she's becoming…
And *that* is powerful.

There's something sacred about the in-between.
It's messy, yes. Uncertain, often. But it's also where the magic is.
Where the breaking turns into building.
Where the questioning births clarity.
Where the pain makes room for power.

The woman I'm becoming no longer
asks for permission to exist.
She doesn't shrink to fit spaces that
can't hold her greatness.
She doesn't silence her voice to
make others comfortable.
She is rooted, rising, and ready.

Becoming doesn't mean you have
it all figured out.
It means you're choosing growth over comfort.
Healing over hiding.
Authenticity over approval.

It means waking up and deciding—
every day—to be a little more *you*.
You're not here by accident.
You're here because something deep within you whispered,
"It's time."

Time to rediscover who you are beneath
the roles, expectations, and noise.
Time to shake off everything that's weighed you down
and rise into your *becoming*.

So ask yourself…
Who is she?
This woman you're becoming?

How does she walk into a room?
How does she protect her peace?
What boundaries does she hold?
What energy does she carry?

Because here's the truth:
You don't *find* her.
You *create* her—
One decision, one lesson, one breakthrough at a time.

Let this chapter be your declaration.
You are not finished.
You are forming.
And you are *phenomenal* in the process.

The woman I'm becoming understands that healing is not linear. Some days feel like light. Others feel like weight. But she keeps going, even when her steps are slow, even when her heart is heavy. Because she knows— every ounce of effort matters. Every small act of self-love is a brick in the foundation of her new life.

> *"You may not control all the events that happen to you, but you can decide not to be reduced by them."*
> — Maya Angelou

She is learning to hold space for all versions of herself—the wounded one, the one who survived, the one who dreamed even in the dark. She honors them. They got her here. But they are no longer in control. She is.

She's rewriting the narrative. Not the one others handed her. Not the one shaped by trauma, fear, or shame. *Her* narrative. Written in bold ink and truth. She is not broken she is rebuilding. There was a time she poured endlessly into everyone else, leaving herself empty. Now? She pours with intention. She pours from a place of overflow. Because she knows: you can't give what you don't have.

The woman I'm becoming is no longer chasing perfection. She's chasing peace. And in doing so, she's realizing that peace often requires letting go of people, of pasts, of patterns. She no longer waits for validation. Her worth isn't up for debate.

There was a time when I based my worth on the applause of others. If they approved, I felt worthy. If they didn't, I questioned everything about myself. I remember once pouring my heart into a project, giving it everything I had—late nights, early mornings, second-guessing every detail just to hear someone say, "Good job." And when they didn't, it crushed me. I didn't realize it then, but I had handed them the pen to write my value. It took time, reflection, and honestly, a lot of tears to understand that validation given externally can be taken away just as quickly. But the kind I give myself? That's mine to keep. Now, I create, I speak, I live—not for applause, but from alignment. That's freedom. She wakes up and decides she is enough. Because she is. Always has been.

> *"Owning our story and loving ourselves through that process is the bravest thing we'll ever do."*
> — Brené Brown

She is soft, but not weak. Strong, but not hard. Loving, but no longer self-sacrificing. She understands that compassion begins at home—with herself. She speaks up. Not just for others, but for herself. She no longer lowers her voice to be accepted. She knows her truth has power. And she uses it.

The woman I'm becoming is not afraid of solitude. She understands that some of the most important growth happens in quiet moments. But I wasn't always that way. I used to fear silence like it was a punishment. I kept myself surrounded—by people, noise, distractions—anything to avoid being alone with my thoughts. I equated solitude with loneliness, and loneliness with failure. If I was by myself, didn't that mean something was wrong with me?

I remember my first real encounter with solitude. It was quiet. Too quiet. I sat on my couch, phone face down, TV off, no music, no distractions—and I hated it. My mind ran wild. Every insecurity, every memory, every "should've" and "what if" came flooding in. I almost gave up.

But something inside whispered, "Stay. Just a little longer." So, I did. And again, the next day. And the next. And slowly, the silence became less of a threat and more of an invitation. I began using that time to journal, pray, meditate—sometimes just to breathe. I didn't realize how much of myself I'd been avoiding.

In that solitude, I met the real me—not the version shaped by others' expectations, but the raw, vulnerable, beautiful woman beneath it all. I learned I'm stronger than I thought. More intuitive than I knew. I uncovered passions, released burdens, and finally heard my own voice.

Solitude became sacred. Not a space of emptiness, but of fullness.

Now, I seek it. Not to escape others—but to return to myself. She doesn't fear being alone—she embraces it, knowing that in stillness, she meets herself.

She walks differently now. With intention. With presence. With grace. And when she looks in the mirror, she doesn't just see a face—she sees a journey. A story unfolding. A legacy in the making.

> *"I am not afraid of storms, for I am learning how to sail my ship."*
> *— Louisa May Alcott*

You are her. She is you. And she's still becoming. Take a breath. Close your eyes. And feel her rising within you. You are not lost. You are not behind. You are on your way.

This is your becoming.

A Prayer for Mental and Spiritual Growth

*God of wisdom and grace,
I come before You with a heart open to change,
A mind ready to expand,
And a spirit yearning to grow deeper in You.*

*Clear the clutter from my thoughts.
Remove the lies I've believed about who I am and what I can't do.
Replace them with truth—Your truth.
Let clarity replace confusion, and peace replace anxiety.*

*Strengthen my mental endurance,
That I may think with purpose, focus, and discernment.
Help me cast down every imagination
That doesn't align with Your will.*

*Feed my spirit with Your Word,
Water it with revelation,
And prune away anything that keeps me from thriving. Let my faith grow roots that anchor me during storms, And wings that lift me when life tries to hold me down.*

*Teach me to be still and listen,
To trust You in silence and act boldly when called.
Stretch me without breaking me,
Challenge me without crushing me.*

*I declare today:
My mind is renewed.
My spirit is awakened.
My life is shifting—upward and forward.
In Jesus' name,
Amen.*

Reflection Prompt:

Describe the woman you are becoming in vivid detail. What does she believe? How does she love, lead, and live? What are you leaving behind in order to become her?

Journaling Space:

Write your personal "I am becoming" statement.

Affirmation

I am becoming the woman of my own vision, led by purpose, shaped by truth, and filled with power.

Chapter 2
Mental and Spiritual Growth: Nurturing Your Inner Power

Look at you, already on Chapter Two!

You made it through Chapter One without throwing the book across the room? That alone deserves a standing ovation and maybe a slice of cake. (No judgment here—I celebrate breakthroughs with dessert.) But seriously, give yourself credit. You just looked yourself in the mirror, peeled back a few layers, and called out the woman you're becoming. That's courageous.

Now, let's talk about what holds her together—what fuels her when the world feels loud, heavy, and just plain exhausting. Your mind and your spirit. That quiet, invisible force that keeps you going even when you feel like giving up. Your inner power.

"You can't pour from an empty cup, and you can't fake a full soul."

Mental and spiritual growth isn't about chanting mantras on a mountain (though that does sound amazing). It's about getting honest. About your thoughts. Your beliefs. Your inner dialogue. It's about nurturing the parts of you no one sees—but that affect everything you do.

I used to think growth had to be loud—like some giant declaration to the world: "LOOK AT ME EVOLVING!" But real growth? It's quiet. It's in the way you talk to yourself when no one's listening. It's how you get back up after the emotional rug's been pulled from under you. It's deciding not to respond to the drama. It's learning to sit still when your instinct is to run.

Let's go there. Let's talk about the mental clutter, the emotional weight, the spiritual droughts—and how we rise from them.

THE POWER OF MINDSET

Your mind is the steering wheel of your life. If your thoughts are constantly spiraling into worry, fear, or doubt, guess what direction you're headed? That's right—straight into burnout boulevard.

But here's the game-changer: you get to choose your thoughts. You get to challenge the ones that tell you you're not enough, not ready, not worthy.

I remember the first time I questioned one of my self-limiting beliefs. I had been telling myself for years, "You're not good at public speaking." But one day, I asked myself, *"Who told you that?"* And honestly, I couldn't come up with a name. It was just a sentence I had adopted and never challenged. So, I did. I practiced. I spoke. I shook. I sweat. And then... I got better.

> *"Whether you think you can or you think you can't, you're right."*
> —Henry Ford

Your mindset is a garden. You have to tend to it. Pull the weeds. Water the truth. Let the sun of self-awareness in. And stop planting seeds of self-doubt.

I also had to break up with perfectionism. Whew—she was a whole toxic relationship! I used to think if everything wasn't perfect, I failed. But I've learned that growth is messy. That sometimes, you have to be okay with showing up with shaking hands and a brave heart. Progress doesn't always look pretty, but it's still progress.

SPIRITUAL GROWTH: GOING DEEPER THAN THE SURFACE

Spiritual growth is like having a GPS for your soul. It's what grounds you when everything else feels unstable. It's that deep-down knowing that there's more to life than what you see. It's faith, it's stillness, it's divine connection.

But let's keep it real: sometimes, spiritual growth starts with a breakdown. It starts when you've tried all the worldly things—people, achievements, distractions—and still feel empty.

For me, it started in a waiting room. Waiting for news that would change everything. I prayed for the first time in a long time. Not the kind of prayer you rehearse—just a raw whisper: *"Help me."* And in that quiet moment, something shifted. Not the situation. Me.

> *"Almost everything will work again if you unplug it for a few minutes... including you."*
> — Anne Lamott

That's when I realized spiritual growth wasn't about always feeling good. It was about being rooted. About finding peace even in the storm.

I started a morning ritual—nothing elaborate. Just a cup of tea, a quiet corner, a short devotional or a scripture, and silence. That silence became holy. It became the space where I met myself and God all over again. Some mornings I cried. Some mornings I laughed. But every morning, I grew.

PRACTICES THAT FUEL INNER POWER

Here's the good news: nurturing your mental and spiritual growth doesn't require a retreat in Bali (though if someone's offering, I'll pack a bag). You can start right where you are. Here are a few things that changed everything for me:

- **Journaling** – Write it all out. The messy, the magical, the mundane. Your journal is your safe space.
- **Prayer & Meditation** – You don't have to be perfect. Just be present. Talk to God, to the universe, to yourself. And then... listen.
- **Affirmations** – Speak life over yourself. Daily. Even when you don't believe it yet.
- **Unplugging** – Sometimes, the most spiritual thing you can do is turn your phone off.
- **Protecting Your Peace** – Say no. Walk away. Guard your mental and emotional energy like its gold—because it is.

> *"You owe yourself the love that*
> *you so freely give to others."*
> *— Alexandra Elle*

I used to think meditation had to be some grand, peaceful moment on a mountaintop. In reality, my meditation looked like five deep breaths in my car before work. Or sitting in silence for ten minutes while the world around me kept spinning. That was enough. That was sacred.

One practice that surprised me was solitude walks. No phone, no podcast, no company—just me and the world. Those walks became a form of moving meditation. With every step, I felt myself shedding stress, quieting the noise, and realigning with truth.

REWRITING THE NARRATIVE

You are not your past. You are not your trauma. You are not your anxious thoughts. You are not the worst thing that's happened to you.

You are a soul with resilience in her bones and wisdom in her spirit. You are learning, growing, becoming.

Every day, you have the chance to rewrite the story. To choose thoughts that empower you. To feed your spirit with truth. To walk like the powerful woman, you are becoming.

> *"You will always belong to yourself. And that is the most beautiful thing."*
> — *Rupi Kaur*

This chapter isn't about perfection. It's about *practice*. And progress. You're not here to perform your growth. You're here to *live* it.

Let's keep nurturing that fire inside you—the one that doesn't burn out, even when life tries to dim it.

A PERSONAL BECOMING MOMENT

I'll never forget the day everything shifted.

It wasn't some movie scene with dramatic background music. There were no fireworks, no sudden lightning bolt of revelation. It was just… a quiet, ordinary afternoon.

I had been drifting through life on autopilot—mentally drained, spiritually disconnected, and emotionally running on fumes. My smile didn't quite reach my eyes anymore, and my soul felt like it was whispering, *"We can't keep going like this."*

That afternoon, I picked up my journal. Not because I was feeling inspired or expecting some big breakthrough, but simply because I had promised myself I would write daily. Honestly, it felt more like checking a box than self-discovery.

I didn't even know where to start, so I wrote the first thing that came to mind:
"I don't know who I am anymore."

The words looked foreign and familiar all at once. I stared at them for a long time.

And then, without even thinking, I wrote the next sentence:
"But I want to find out."

That one line cracked something open inside me. I felt tears slide down my cheeks—not tears of pain, but of release. In that moment, I realized I had been carrying so much weight—expectations, responsibilities, the need to be "the strong one"—that I never stopped to truly meet myself.

That moment wasn't about "fixing" me. It was about *finding* me.

It was a turning point, because here's what I learned: mental and spiritual growth doesn't always start with a grand transformation. Sometimes, it starts with a whisper. A small decision to stop numbing, stop running, and simply *be* with yourself long enough to listen.

From that day forward, I approached my life differently. I prayed more—not to get answers instantly, but to feel God's presence guiding me. I asked myself better questions. I stopped avoiding silence and instead made friends with it. I realized that mental clarity and spiritual peace weren't luxuries—they were lifelines.

And slowly, I began to rise—not because my circumstances had changed, but because *I* had changed.

Your growth will look different from mine, but I promise you this: you don't need to be perfect, fixed, or have it all figured out to start. You just need to be willing to say, *"I want to find out who I really am."*

That willingness is the seed. Water it daily—with grace, patience, and honesty—and watch your life bloom.

A Prayer for Mental and Spiritual Growth

Dear God,

Help me quiet the noise in my mind and soften the weight on my spirit.

Remind me that I am never alone, even when I feel disconnected.

Teach me to trust the process of becoming, even when I don't understand it.

Give me the strength to release thoughts that do not serve me, and the courage to replace them with truth.

Let your peace guide me, your wisdom shape me, and your love root me deeply.

Amen.

Reflection Prompt:

What thoughts have you been carrying that no longer serve the woman you're becoming? What can you replace them with?

Journaling Space:

Create a daily affirmation practice. Write 5 affirmations that speak life, power, and truth over your mind and spirit.

Affirmation

I protect my mind. I nurture my spirit. I grow daily into the highest, truest version of myself.

Chapter 3
Unlearning the Lies

Okay, let's be honest, this chapter might step on a few toes... including yours. But that's only because we're about to snatch some dusty old beliefs off the shelf and hold them up to the light like, "Wait... why was I even believing that?" Think of this as mental spring cleaning. Buckle up—it's time to declutter your mind.

You know what's wild? Some of the hardest things to let go of aren't toxic people they're toxic beliefs.

And many of them aren't even yours.

You inherited them. Absorbed them. Got handed them by parents, culture, religion, teachers, relationships, or society like a junky hand-me-down sweater that you kept wearing—because someone told you it looked good.

But just because it was given to you doesn't mean you have to keep it.

> *"You are not responsible for the programming*
> *you received as a child. But as an adult,*
> *you are responsible for upgrading it."*
> *—Unknown*

This chapter is all about cleaning house. It's time to open the windows, air out the stale narratives, and get honest about what beliefs are actually *true*—and which ones have simply been living rent-free in your head for far too long.

THE LIES WE TELL OURSELVES (AND WHERE THEY CAME FROM)

Here are just a few familiar ones:

- "I have to earn love."
- "If I'm not productive, I'm not valuable."
- "Other people's comfort matters more than my truth."
- "My worth is tied to how much I give."
- "If I speak up, I'll be rejected."
- "I have to be strong all the time."

Sound familiar?

These messages may have helped you survive a season, but now they're keeping you from thriving.

Sometimes, these beliefs aren't even spoken aloud. They're passed down in how we were treated, what was praised or punished, and what was modeled for us.

If you saw your mother run herself ragged to make everyone happy, you probably believed your value is in what you *do*, not who you *are*.

If your vulnerability was met with shame, you may have learned to silence yourself to feel safe.

If no one ever told you that your dreams were valid—you may have learned to shrink them down so they wouldn't disappoint you later.

But now? Now you get to choose differently.

The Power of Unlearning

Unlearning is not about blame—it's about awareness. You get to hold compassion for how you learned it *and* courage for unlearning it.

It's the moment you say:

- "This belief might've protected me before—but now it's blocking my growth."
- "That rule helped me stay small. I'm not doing that anymore."
- "Just because I was taught it doesn't mean I have to carry it."

> *"The most powerful thing you can do is question the story you've been told about who you are."*
> *—Danielle LaPorte*

Unlearning requires honesty, patience, and grace. It's peeling off labels that never belonged to you in the first place.

It's also about choosing love over fear. Every time.

A Personal Becoming Moment

One of the biggest lies I had to unlearn was that needing help made me weak.

I grew up thinking that strong meant silent. That asking for help was admitting failure. So, I carried everything on my own until I broke under the weight of pretending.

The first time I said, "I can't do this by myself," I felt like I was betraying the version of me that had powered through everything. But you know what actually happened?

I healed. Faster. Deeper. Better.

Unlearning that lie gave me access to real connection, to real support, and to a version of myself that didn't have to pretend to be superhuman.

There was power in that surrender. And peace in that honesty.

Another lie I had to unlearn? That I had to earn rest.

I used to push myself to exhaustion, thinking productivity was proof of worth. If I wasn't doing something "useful," I felt guilty.

But here's what I've come to believe: rest is holy. Rest is wise. Rest is fuel. And I am not a machine.

Now, when I rest, I call it a radical act of rebellion. A declaration that I am already enough—even when I'm not producing.

How to Start Unlearning

1. Name the belief. What's the lie you've been living by?
2. Trace the root. Where did it come from? Who gave it to you?
3. Question its truth. Is it serving you? Is it true 100% of the time?
4. Replace it. What new belief do you want to live by instead?

For example:

- Old Belief: "I'm too emotional."
- New Truth: "My emotions are valid and make me human."
- Old Belief: "I have to earn my place."
- New Truth: "I belong simply because I exist."
- Old Belief: "I must be strong all the time."
- New Truth: "My softness is sacred, too."

Unlearning is a practice. Sometimes, those old voices will still creep in. But the more you practice choosing truth, the quieter they become.

Let's Talk About Cultural Lies

Some lies are deeply woven into the culture around us:

- Hustle culture tells you rest is laziness.
- Diet culture tells you your body must shrink to be worthy.
- Beauty culture tells you aging is something to be fixed.
- Gender roles tell you what you "should" be doing with your life.

We've been swimming in these messages for so long that we don't always see them. But once you do—you can't unsee them.

Awareness is the first act of freedom.

THE EMOTIONAL WEIGHT OF UNLEARNING

Here's something we don't talk about enough: unlearning can be *grieving*.

Grieving the years spent living a lie. Grieving the version of you that didn't know better. Grieving the relationships that only survived because of your silence.

Let yourself feel that.

Let yourself say, "I wish I knew then what I know now." And then offer yourself grace.

You did the best you could with what you had. And now, you get to choose differently.

Affirmations to Rewrite the Script

- I do not have to earn rest, love, or joy.
- I am allowed to take up space and speak my truth.
- I am not here to shrink or perform.
- I release the beliefs that no longer serve me.
- I am writing new truths rooted in freedom.
- My story is mine to rewrite.
- I honor who I've been and celebrate who I'm becoming.

A Prayer for Release and Renewal

Dear God,

Thank You for the strength to question what I've been taught and the wisdom to seek what is true.

Help me unlearn every lie that has kept me small, quiet, or afraid.

Show me the truth of who I am in You—free, whole, and deeply loved.

Let my life be led by freedom, not fear. And when old beliefs rise up again, remind me that I've been set free.

Renew my mind daily. Teach me how to walk in truth and live in light.

Amen.

Reflection Prompt:

What is a lie you were taught (directly or indirectly) that you now recognize as false? How has it shaped your life?

Bonus Prompt:

What would your life look like if you fully believed the *opposite* of that lie?

Journaling Space:

Rewrite that belief in your own words. Replace it with a truth that feels loving, grounded, and free. Write it again and again until it feels like yours.

Affirmation

I am not bound by old beliefs. I choose truth. I choose freedom. I am unlearning and becoming.

Chapter 4
Take the Time to Get to Know Yourself

Here's a radical thought: what if you made yourself your favorite person to be around?

I know, I know—some of us barely like hearing our own voicemail greeting, let alone hanging out with ourselves. But hear me out: what if getting to know yourself was less like a therapy session and more like a girls' trip with the most intriguing person you've never fully explored? Spoiler: she's already living rent-free in your mirror.

We spend so much of our lives getting to know other people—their love languages, their pet peeves, their dreams. We ask questions, we lean in, we remember details. But how often do we do that for ourselves?

This chapter is your invitation to slow down and really meet the person you see in the mirror. Because the truth is: you cannot love what you do not know. And you cannot become who you're meant to be if you're still a stranger to yourself.

> *"Knowing yourself is the beginning of all wisdom."*
> *— Aristotle*

Why Self-Knowledge Matters

When you know yourself, you stop settling. You stop shapeshifting to fit rooms that weren't built for you. You make decisions that align with your truth. You stop asking for directions to places your soul already knows how to find.

Knowing yourself means understanding what fuels you, what drains you, what triggers you, and what lights you up. It's about naming your patterns and breaking the ones that no longer serve you.

And most of all—it's about choosing to be curious, not critical.

Self-knowledge is the root of self-trust. When you truly know yourself, you stop second-guessing your instincts. You move with clarity. You speak with conviction. You live with intention.

> *"At the center of you being you have the answer; you know who you are and you know what you want."*
> — Lao Tzu

Who Am I, Really?

It's a scary question, isn't it?

We often attach our identity to roles—mom, wife, leader, caretaker. And while those roles are meaningful, they are not the whole of you.

Who are you when no one is watching? Who are you when there's nothing to prove?

Start with the basics:

- What do I love?
- What do I need?
- What do I believe?
- What makes me feel most like me?

These aren't questions with one-time answers. They evolve as you do.

A Personal Becoming Moment

There was a season when I realized I didn't really know myself anymore. I had spent so many years focused on everyone else—being who I needed to be, showing up how others expected me to—that I lost track of my own reflection.

So, I made a commitment: every morning, before the world got access to me, I'd check in with myself. Sometimes that meant journaling. Sometimes it meant dancing in my kitchen. Sometimes it meant just sitting in silence.

And slowly, I started remembering.

I remembered that I love sunrises. That writing helps me breathe. That silence doesn't mean emptiness it means space.

That rediscovery wasn't a straight line. But it brought me back to myself. And from that place? Everything changed.

One morning, I wrote a letter to myself. It started with, "Hey you. I've missed you." That was the first time I felt tears of reunion. I wasn't just surviving anymore I was reconnecting.

SIMPLE WAYS TO GET TO KNOW YOURSELF

- Journal honestly. Not for perfection—just truth.
- Try new things. See what sparks something inside you.
- Unplug regularly. Let your own voice be the loudest.
- Ask yourself powerful questions. And answer without judgment.
- Date yourself. Take yourself out. Spend intentional time with you.
- Celebrate your quirks. The weird, beautiful, uniquely-you things that make you.

"You owe yourself the love, time, and attention that you so freely give to others."
— *Unknown*

A Prayer for Self-Discovery

Dear God,

Thank You for creating me with purpose, passion, and personality.

Help me to peel back the layers I've put on to survive and get back to the essence of who You made me to be.

Guide me to explore with grace, to embrace with love, and to discover with courage.

When I forget who I am, remind me. When I'm afraid of what I'll find, walk with me.

Let this journey back to myself be filled with revelation, freedom, and joy.

Amen.

Reflection Prompt:

What is something you recently discovered or remembered about yourself? How did it feel to come home to that truth?

Journaling Space:

Write a letter to yourself—your truest self. Tell her what you love about her.

Affirmation

I am worth knowing, loving, and understanding. I choose to meet myself with curiosity and compassion.

Chapter 5
The Power of Vulnerability

Let's get honest: being vulnerable feels like showing up to a party in your pajamas while everyone else is wearing armor.

(And let's be real—your pajamas are probably fabulous, but still.)

Vulnerability has been branded as weakness for too long. We've been taught to keep it together, be strong, don't cry, don't let them see you sweat. So, what do we do? We smile through pain, make jokes out of trauma, and call it "being fine."

But guess what? "Fine" has a breaking point.

> *"Owning our story and loving ourselves through that process is the bravest thing we'll ever do."*
> —Brené Brown

Vulnerability is a Strength, not a Symptom

It takes courage to be seen when you're still healing. It takes heart to open up when you don't have all the answers. Vulnerability isn't weakness—it's truth in motion. And when you share your truth, you give others permission to do the same.

It's in vulnerability that relationships deepen. That walls fall. That real healing begins.

And yes, it's scary. But it's also freeing. Being vulnerable is like opening a window and letting the fresh air in. It can feel awkward at first, even risky—but it allows what's real to breathe.

WHY WE HIDE (AND HOW IT HURTS US)

We hide because we're scared of being judged, rejected, or misunderstood.

We hide because we think we have to be the strong one.

We hide because we were taught that emotions are messy—and messy is bad.

But here's what I've learned: hiding doesn't protect your heart—it starves it.

When you hide long enough, even *you* forget who you are underneath the mask. Vulnerability is how you find your way back. It's not about oversharing or being dramatic—it's about being honest. First with yourself. Then with others.

"You don't have to be fearless—just willing."

Some of the strongest people I know are the ones who say, "I'm not okay right now." Not because they're falling apart—but because they're brave enough to be seen as they are.

A PERSONAL BECOMING MOMENT

There was a time I was barely holding it together. My heart felt heavy, my mind was exhausted, and my smile—if you could even call it that—was hanging on by a thread.

But I had made a promise to someone that I would show up. And so I did.

Here's the difference: that day, I didn't try to put on the "I'm fine" mask. I didn't paint over my emotions with polite smiles or small talk. I walked in just as I was—no filters, no performance, no pretending.

I expected awkwardness. I expected people to pull back. Instead, something beautiful happened.

Afterward, someone came up to me and said, *"You have no idea how much I needed to see someone be real today."*

That moment shifted something deep inside me. I realized that my cracks weren't flaws to be hidden—they were invitations for connection. By showing my unpolished, unedited self, I gave someone else the permission they didn't even know they were waiting for: permission to breathe.

It made me wonder—how many of us are holding our breath around each other, desperately hoping for a sign that it's okay to exhale?

Vulnerability is that sign.

It's not weakness—it's courage in its purest form. It's the quiet power of saying, *"This is me, right now, as I am."* It's trusting that even in your not-so-perfect moments, you are still worthy of love, respect, and belonging.

That day taught me that people aren't inspired by our perfection—they're inspired by our presence. They connect to our humanity, not our highlight reel.

So if you're reading this and wondering if you're "too much" or "not enough," hear me: you are exactly what someone needs to see today. Your realness might be the light that breaks someone else's darkness.

How We Confuse Vulnerability with Weakness

Here's what vulnerability is *not*:

- It's not spilling your secrets to anyone with ears.
- It's not crying in public just to prove you feel deeply.
- It's not performing your pain.

It's about presence. It's about truth. It's about showing up as your full, beautiful, flawed, healing self—even when you'd rather hide.

Being vulnerable is admitting that yes, you've been through some things—but you're still here, still learning, still becoming. That's strength in motion.

> *"To share your weakness is to make yourself vulnerable; to make yourself vulnerable is to show your strength."*
> —Criss Jami

Practicing Vulnerability Without Losing Yourself

Boundaries are what keep vulnerability safe. You can be vulnerable and still have standards. You can share your truth and still protect your peace. Vulnerability isn't about being wide open all the time—it's about being *authentically open* in the right spaces.

Here's how to keep it sacred:

- **Choose your people.** Not everyone has earned access to your heart.
- **Know your limits.** You're allowed to say, "I'm not ready to talk about that."
- **Check your motives.** Are you sharing to connect or to be rescued?
- **Protect your healing.** Some stories are still in progress—and that's okay.

When Vulnerability Becomes a Superpower

When you lead with honesty, you attract others who do the same. When you model grace for your own growth, you make it okay for others to grow too.

Your vulnerability can open doors that armor never could. It can disarm tension, soften conflict, deepen intimacy, and shift atmospheres.

The truth is, we all long to be seen—but someone has to go first. Someone has to say, "I don't have it all together" so others can finally breathe.

Let it be you.

Everyday Moments to Be Vulnerable

You don't need a TED Talk moment to practice vulnerability. It happens in the small, honest decisions you make every day:

- Saying, "I'm struggling" instead of "I'm fine."
- Admitting you don't know instead of pretending.
- Letting someone help you without guilt.
- Telling a friend you need space—and trusting they'll still love you.

The more you practice, the easier it gets. Vulnerability builds muscle. And every time you show up in truth, you build strength.

A Prayer for Courageous Vulnerability

Dear God,

Thank You for creating me with depth and feeling. Teach me that softness is strength. Help me trust that I am safe to be seen.

When I want to shut down, show me how to stay open. When I want to pretend, give me the courage to be real.

May my vulnerability not just heal me, but help someone else feel less alone.

Remind me that even in my most fragile moments, I am held by You.

Amen.

Reflection Prompt:

When was the last time you let yourself be truly seen—messy, emotional, and real? How did it feel?

Bonus Prompt:

What fear comes up for you when you think about being vulnerable? Where did that fear come from—and is it still serving you?

Journaling Space:

Write about a part of you that's been hidden. What would it look like to let her come forward with compassion?

Affirmation

I am safe to be seen. I am strong in my softness. I choose to show up fully, even when it's hard.

My vulnerability is not my flaw—it's my superpower.

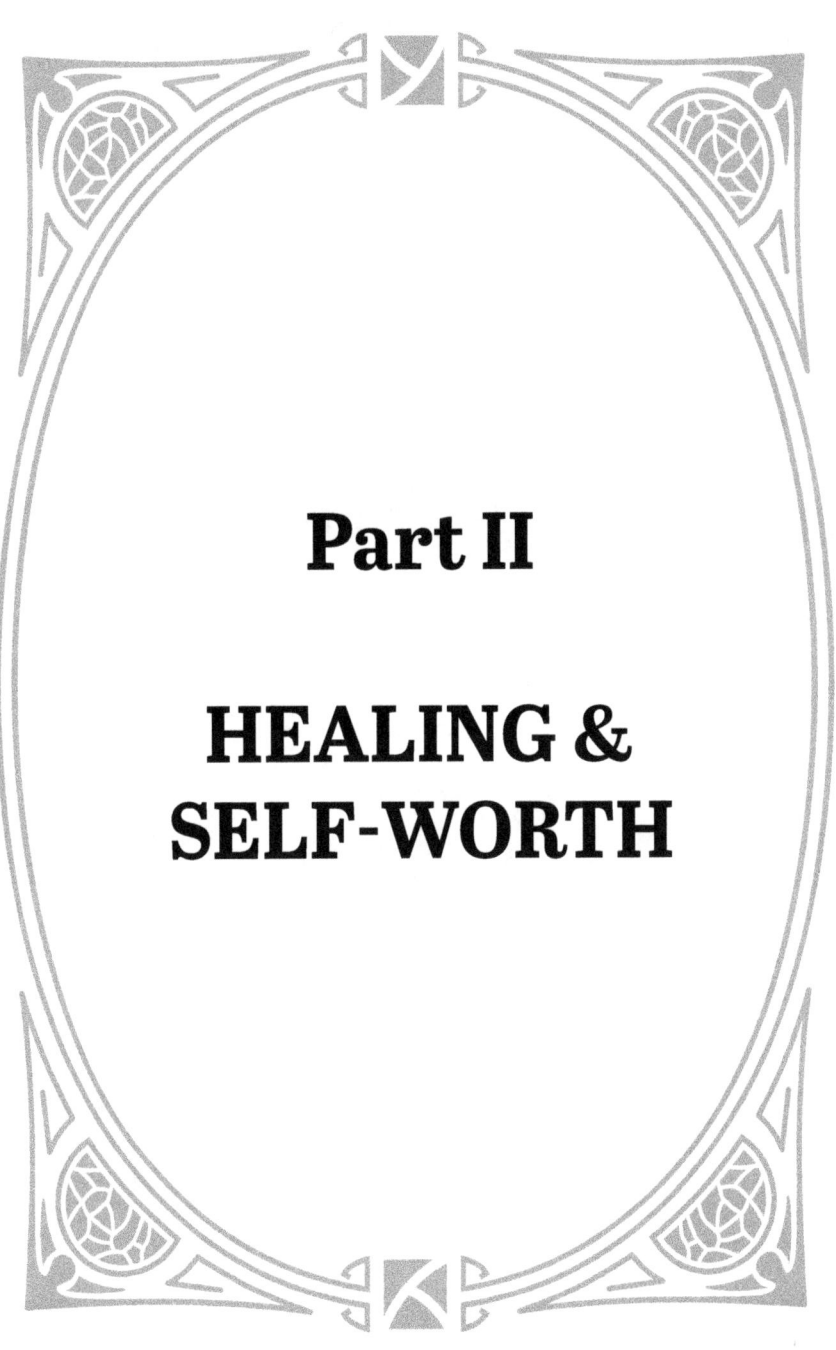

Part II

HEALING & SELF-WORTH

Chapter 6
Love Deprived

You ever notice how you can spot a "love-deprived" person in a crowd? It's not just the lonely sigh or the way they stare too long at couples holding hands. No—sometimes it's the grocery cart that gives it away. Three bottles of wine, a single pint of ice cream (that we're pretending will last the week), and a scented candle labeled *"Warm Embrace"*. Girl, I've been there. In fact, I've been the CEO, CFO, and marketing director of the Love-Deprived Association—unofficial membership perks included scrolling dating apps at 2 a.m. and making questionable decisions about text messages.

THE EMOTIONAL DIVE

But here's the thing: love deprivation isn't always about romance. It's about the aching space where connection, affirmation, and belonging *should* live—but don't. It's the invisible hunger we try to satisfy with busy schedules, excessive generosity, or pouring ourselves into relationships that give us crumbs and call it a meal.

I remember lying in bed one night, staring at the ceiling, feeling like my heart had been in a drought for years. People knew my name, loved my laugh, and even leaned on me for advice—but none of it touched that empty place inside. It wasn't that I didn't have people around me… it was that I didn't feel *chosen*. And that's a whole different kind of loneliness.

THE COURAGE TO NAME IT

Here's the courageous part: I had to stop pretending I was okay. I had to say out loud, "I feel unloved." Those words tasted strange in my mouth, like I was betraying the strong woman image I worked so hard to keep. But the truth was, I wasn't just strong. I was tired. Tired of hoping someone would see me without me having to scream. Tired of masking need with a smile. Tired of mistaking attention for love.

A Personal Becoming Moment

It hit me on an ordinary Tuesday.

I was sitting in my car outside the grocery store—hands still on the steering wheel, engine running—just... paused. My cart was empty, but my heart felt even emptier. I had gone there for almond milk and, if I'm honest, probably another candle I didn't need, because candles had become my version of comfort.

But as I sat there, watching people walk in and out, arms full of groceries, kids pulling at their sleeves, I felt a truth rising in my chest that I could no longer avoid:

I had been waiting. Waiting for someone to see me. Waiting for someone to pour into me. Waiting for someone to love me in a way I'd been starving for my whole life.

And then—like a whisper from somewhere deep within—it hit me:

No one is coming.

Not in the way I had imagined. Not in the way I had been secretly hoping. And that wasn't tragedy—it was truth. Because the rescue I had been waiting for? That was *me*.

I had been holding out for a savior, when in reality, I was the one I'd been waiting for all along.

That moment changed me.

I made myself a promise right there in that parking lot, still holding my keys: I would never again make my sense of worth dependent on someone else's willingness—or inability—to give me love. I was done waiting for scraps when I could serve myself a feast.

So I started small.

Every time I felt that hollow ache, every time the old lie whispered, *"You're not enough unless someone says so,"* I did something tangible to show myself love:

- I wrote myself handwritten notes and tucked them into my purse, so I could find them on hard days.
- I took myself on solo coffee dates, sitting there without my phone, just… being with me.
- I buy myself flowers every 2 weeks. I place them at the front door so it's the first thing I see when I step into my home. It's a reminder that I am worthy.

And with every small act, I was telling myself the thing I had waited so long to hear:
I see you.
I choose you.
I love you.

It wasn't about replacing someone else's love. It was about building a foundation so solid that when love from others did come, it was an addition—not a lifeline.

Because the truth is, love deprivation isn't just about who didn't show up for you—it's about how long you've been abandoning yourself.

And I decided that day, in the front seat of my car, that I would never leave me again.

PASSIONATE TRUTH

If you've been love deprived, let me tell you something radical: you can fill your own cup without apology. The day I stopped treating self-love like a consolation prize and started treating it like the main event, my life shifted. Love started showing up—not because I was desperate for it, but because I had become a magnet for it.

A Prayer for Courage

God, give me the courage to admit when I'm empty, the wisdom to stop looking for my worth in someone else's hands, and the grace to love myself the way You love me—fully, fiercely, and without condition.

Let me walk in the truth that I am already chosen.

Amen

Reflection Prompt:

Think about a time you felt unloved or overlooked.

What did you tell yourself about your worth in that moment?

Did you try to fill that gap with other people, distractions, or busyness?

How would you respond differently today, knowing what you now know about loving yourself first?

Journaling Space:

Write a love letter to yourself — not for who you *wish* you were, but for exactly who you are right now.

- Thank yourself for surviving the seasons where love felt scarce.
- Celebrate the parts of you that no one else has fully seen or appreciated.
- Declare how you will choose to love and honor yourself moving forward, without waiting for someone else to do it first.

Affirmation

I am not defined by the love I did
or did not receive from others.

I am whole, worthy, and overflowing
with love from within.

I choose to give myself the care, respect,
and affection I once waited for.

Chapter 7
Learning to Love Yourself First

Let's get something straight: loving yourself isn't arrogance—it's alignment.

We're not talking about becoming the person who only posts selfies with inspirational quotes (unless that's your vibe—in which case, slay on). This is deeper. It's about learning to like the woman you see in the mirror—even before coffee and after a cry.

It's not about thinking you're better than anyone else. It's about knowing you're not less. It's about reclaiming all the pieces of you that life, loss, and people tried to convince you were unworthy. Loving yourself first is not optional—it's foundational.

> *"You alone are enough. You have nothing to prove to anybody."*
> —Maya Angelou

When you love yourself first, everything shifts. Your standards rise. Your peace deepens. Your decisions become rooted, not reactive. You start showing up in your relationships, your work, your life—not from a place of emptiness, but from overflow.

THE LIES WE'VE BEEN TOLD

We've been taught to put everyone else first. To be the helper. The fixer. The strong one. And yes, caring for others is beautiful—but not when it comes at the cost of abandoning ourselves.

You are not selfish for prioritizing your healing. You are not dramatic for having needs. You are not arrogant for choosing to love yourself.

You are whole, even while becoming.

What Loving Yourself Looks Like

It's not always bubble baths and spa days (though those are great too). Sometimes, it's doing the hard thing:

- Walking away from someone who doesn't respect you.
- Saying no to opportunities that don't align.
- Forgiving yourself for what you didn't know then.
- Speaking kindly to yourself, especially on the hard days.
- Choosing rest over proving your worth through productivity.

> *"Talk to yourself like you would to someone you love."*
> —Brené Brown

A Personal Becoming Moment

There was a time I could pour love into everyone around me like I was a bottomless fountain—but when it came to me? Bone dry.

One morning, I stood in front of the mirror and couldn't even look myself in the eyes. It wasn't because I didn't have makeup on, or my hair wasn't "done." It was deeper than that. I realized I had been celebrating everyone else's wins, showing up for everyone else's needs, but completely neglecting the person staring back at me.

So, I decided to start small.

Each morning, I'd stand in front of that same mirror and say, *"You're doing the best you can. I love you."* At first, it felt awkward—like I was rehearsing for a role I didn't believe I'd been cast for. But I kept going.

Then, something shifted. One morning, without even thinking, I looked in the mirror and said, *"Girl... you sexy thing, you!"* And I laughed. Not the fake "let's get through this" laugh—the deep, belly laugh that comes from realizing, *Dang, I really am something special.*

So, I took it further. I started talking to myself the way I'd hype up my best friend:

"You are WORTHY."
"You are doing amazing."
"Anyone who gets to know you is blessed."
"You are not for sale, you are priceless."

Over time, something even more powerful happened—my inner voice softened. My self-trust grew. And I stopped apologizing for the way I took up space in this world.

Loving yourself first doesn't mean you love others less. It means you've finally realized you're worthy of the same energy, time, and tenderness you so freely give away.

And here's the kicker: once I started treating myself like someone I actually cared about, everything else changed. My relationships got healthier. My boundaries got stronger. And my joy? My joy overflowed.

So if no one has told you today—*you sexy thing, you*—you are worthy, you are enough, and you deserve to be loved by the person in the mirror first.

One day, I stood in front of the mirror and couldn't look myself in the eyes. I realized I had been showing love to everyone but the person staring back at me.

So, I started small.

Each morning, I'd look in the mirror and say, "You're doing the best you can. I love you." At first, it felt awkward—even silly. But over time, that affirmation became a lifeline. My inner voice softened. My self-trust grew. And I started treating myself like someone I actually cared about.

That changed everything.

SIMPLE WAYS TO PRACTICE SELF-LOVE DAILY

- Affirm yourself out loud. Don't wait for others to validate you.
- Set boundaries without guilt. Your time, your energy, your rules.
- Feed your body nourishing things. Food, movement, rest.
- Let go of comparison. Your lane. Your pace. Your path.
- Celebrate yourself. Loudly. Frequently. Without apology.

A Prayer for Self-Love and Wholeness

Dear God,

Thank You for creating me with intention and beauty. Teach me to see myself through Your eyes—worthy, whole, and deeply loved.

Help me to silence the voices that shame and compare. Remind me that I am enough, exactly as I am.

Let my self-love be rooted in truth, and let that love guide every choice I make.

Amen.

Reflection Prompt:

What has been your biggest barrier to loving yourself fully? How can you begin to shift that narrative?

Journaling Space:

Write a love letter to yourself. Make it raw, real, and kind. Say the things you've always wanted to hear.

Affirmation

I am deeply worthy of love—especially my own. I choose to love myself first, fully, and without apology.

Chapter 8
Learning to Say "No"

This might be the shortest word in the English language—but for many of us, it's also the heaviest.

It's just two letters, but somehow, it's scarier than a group text that says "we need to talk." You know what I mean. Saying no can feel like you're auditioning for a role in someone's disappointment saga. But plot twist—you're actually setting yourself free.

"No."

It can feel like rejection, confrontation, disappointment, or selfishness all wrapped into one syllable. But here's what I want you to understand: saying no isn't about shutting people out—it's about showing up for yourself.

"No is a complete sentence." — Anne Lamott

When you say no to what drains you, distracts you, or disrespects you, you say yes to peace, purpose, and presence. And that's not selfish—it's sacred.

The Blunt Truth

Here's the thing—every "yes" you say out of guilt is a "no" to yourself. Every time you agree to something you don't want to do, you're teaching people that your time, your energy, and your peace are negotiable. And once people know your boundaries are up for debate, guess what? They'll *debate them*.

You have to get comfortable with the fact that not everyone is going to like your boundaries. And that's fine. You're not building a fan club—you're building a life.

Why Saying No Is So Hard

We're conditioned to be nice. To please. To avoid conflict. We don't want to hurt feelings, burn bridges, or seem ungrateful. And so, we overextend. We agree to things with a smile but carry them with resentment.

But what's the cost of that yes?

Every yes that isn't aligned is a no to something that *is*—your rest, your dreams, your priorities, your healing.

The Power Behind the No

No is a boundary. No is clarity. No is a form of protection.

And here's a truth that shifted everything for me: people who truly love and respect you will survive your no. The only people who get offended by your boundaries are the ones who benefited from you not having any.

I remember the first time I said no to something that felt like an obligation. It was terrifying. My voice shook. My heart raced. But afterward, I felt something I hadn't in a long time—*freedom*.

"Every time you say yes to something, you say no to something else. Choose wisely." — Unknown

Say No with Confidence and Compassion

- "Thank you for thinking of me, but I can't commit to that right now."
- "That's not something I have capacity for at the moment."
- "I'm focusing on other priorities right now. I hope you understand."
- "No, but I appreciate you asking."

You don't need a 10-point explanation. Your time, energy, and peace are reason enough.

A Tool for Practicing Your No: The Boundary Filter

Before you say yes, pause and run the request through this quick filter:

1. **Does this align with my current priorities or goals?**
2. **Do I have the energy to do this well and joyfully?**
3. **Am I saying yes out of obligation, fear, or guilt?**
4. **Will saying yes to this mean saying no to something more important?**

If your answers reveal hesitation or misalignment, consider this your sign: a graceful no may serve you—and others—better in the long run.

A Personal Moment of Choosing Me

I was invited to speak at an event that, a few years ago, I would've bent over backwards to attend. I mean—lights, audience, microphone? Old me would've been flattered, hyped, and already picking out my outfit before the invitation hit my inbox.

But when the request came, I was in a very different place in life—a season of deep healing. I didn't need the spotlight. I didn't need another round of "smile and perform." I needed stillness. Quiet. Peace.

Here's the thing most people don't tell you: saying "no" doesn't just feel uncomfortable at first—it can make you feel like you're breaking some unspoken rule. We're taught from a young age to be agreeable, to not ruffle feathers, to show up even when we're running on fumes. But here's the truth: *overextending yourself is not loyalty—it's self-abandonment.*

So when that invitation came, I sat with it. I could feel the part of me that still wanted to say yes out of habit. But then I thought about the version of me I'm becoming—the one who values alignment over applause. And I knew the answer.

No.

Not "No, but maybe next time."

Not "No, but I'll send someone else."

Just—**No.**

I said it with my chest. No long-winded excuses. No guilt-drenched paragraphs to "soften the blow." Just a clear, respectful boundary.

And guess what? The world didn't crumble. The opportunity didn't evaporate forever. That "no" didn't slam a door—it opened one. A door to deeper trust with myself.

Every "no" rooted in self-respect is a "yes" to your peace, your health, and your purpose. And if someone can't handle that? That's their problem to manage, not yours.

So, repeat after me:

No.
No is a full sentence.
No is not up for debate.
No is holy ground.

A Prayer for Courage and Clarity

Dear God,

Help me to recognize when a yes is coming from fear instead of alignment.

Give me the wisdom to know my limits, the courage to honor them, and the peace to stand firm in my no.

Remind me that protecting my energy is an act of love—not just for myself, but for those I serve.

Thank You for the strength to speak truth, set boundaries, and live with intention.

Amen.

Reflection Prompt:

Where in your life have you been saying yes when your heart is saying no? What would it feel like to choose yourself instead?

Journaling Space:

Write down three scenarios where you will practice saying no with confidence and kindness.

Affirmation

I give myself permission to say no without guilt and yes without regret.

Chapter 9
Be Selfish About Your Time

Let's go ahead and say it: being "selfish" with your time is not a bad thing. It's a *bold*, necessary act of self-respect.

And no, that doesn't mean turning into a diva or ghosting your group chat (unless that chat is draining your soul—then maybe reconsider). Think of it as becoming the CEO of your own energy. Your calendar is not community property—it's a sacred scroll.

Your time is your life currency. And yet, so often, we give it away like it's unlimited—like we'll always have more energy, more capacity, more hours. But you don't. And that's not to scare you—it's to *free* you.

You don't owe everyone access to you. You don't have to attend every event, answer every call, or explain why your time is sacred.

> *"Don't get so busy making a living that you forget to make a life."*
> — Dolly Parton

This chapter is your reminder that you have the right to protect your schedule like your peace depends on it—because it does.

TIME AS A REFLECTION OF VALUES

What you prioritize with your time is often what you value most. So, if you're constantly spending hours on things that drain you or serve someone else's vision—what does that say about where you're placing your worth?

Being intentional with your time isn't just about productivity. It's about alignment. It's about making sure the life you say you want is reflected in how you're spending your minutes, hours, and days.

"How you spend your time is how you spend your life."

The Guilt Trap

One of the biggest barriers to being selfish with your time? Guilt. That lingering voice that says, "If I don't do it, who will?" or "They'll think I don't care."

But here's what I learned: people who love and respect you will also respect your boundaries. The ones who get upset when you choose yourself were never benefitting from your boundaries—they were benefitting from your lack of them.

I used to say yes out of habit. Yes, to things I didn't want to do. Yes, to things that stole my peace. Until one day, I realized my calendar was full—but my spirit was empty.

That's when I started practicing the sacred art of *selective availability*. And let me tell you: peace looks good on me.

Practical Boundaries to Reclaim Your Time

- **Set "you" hours.** Block out time that is strictly for your own rest, reflection, or joy.
- **Pause before responding.** Give yourself permission to check in before committing.

- **Practice "soft no's."** A kind no is still a no.
- **Communicate with clarity.** You don't need to over-explain. "I'm not available" is a complete sentence.
- **Audit your calendar.** What's filling your days—and does it reflect your dreams?

"When you say yes to others, make sure you're not saying no to yourself." — Paulo Coelho

A Personal Becoming Moment: Boundary Breakthrough

There was a week when my calendar looked like a war zone. Three events lined up back-to-back: a work obligation I couldn't wriggle out of, a friend's birthday dinner, and a community event I had been "volunteered" for.

I said yes to all three—not because I had the energy, but because I felt guilty saying no. I told myself, *They're counting on you. It's just one evening. You'll be fine.*

But I wasn't fine. By the time Sunday rolled around, I felt like my soul had been scraped raw. I sat in my living room—lights off, phone on silent—and I cried. Not because of any single event, but because I realized something heartbreaking: I had betrayed myself.

I had abandoned my own needs to show up for everyone else's. I had given away my time and my energy like it was on clearance, without considering the cost to my well-being.

And that's when it hit me: time is the most precious currency I have, and I was spending it recklessly.

From that moment on, I made a promise to myself.

If I needed rest, I would take it.

If something didn't align with my values or my energy, I would decline—without over-explaining, without guilt.

And do you know what happened?

The world didn't fall apart. My relationships didn't crumble. My friends didn't disown me. In fact, something unexpected happened—my relationships got *healthier*. Because when I did show up, I wasn't dragging my tired body and empty spirit along for the ride. I was present. I was engaged. I was *me*.

Here's the thing: being selfish with your time isn't about hoarding it. It's about *protecting it*. It's about understanding that your "yes" means nothing if it's draining the life out of you.

So, from here on out, I want you to hear me loud and clear—your peace is worth more than someone's temporary disappointment. And every time you choose yourself, you're not being selfish… you're being wise.

A Prayer for Discernment and Boundaries

Dear God,

Help me to steward my time with wisdom, clarity, and intention.

Teach me that rest is not a reward, but a rhythm.

Give me the courage to say no without guilt, and the strength to say yes only when it aligns with my purpose.

Let me honor the gift of time You've given me by using it in ways that bring peace, growth, and joy.

Amen.

Reflection Prompt:

Where are you spending time that feels misaligned with your values or energy? What can you begin to let go of?

Journaling Space:

Create a "time boundary" list—what you will no longer accept, and what you want to make more room for.

Affirmation

My time is valuable. I protect it boldly,
use it wisely, and honor it with purpose.

Chapter 10
Pour Into Yourself Before You Pour into Others

If no one has told you today: you deserve your own love, too.

This might be the chapter where you're tempted to skip ahead and keep giving to everyone else—but hold up. If your phones at 1% battery, you plug it in, right? So why do we treat ourselves like we can run on spiritual fumes and cold coffee forever? Let's fix that.

Yes, you—the giver, the fixer, the peacemaker. The one always checking in on everyone else. You've been showing up, holding space, and pouring your heart out like it's an infinite well. But sis, even the strongest cup runs empty when it's never refilled.

This chapter is your permission slip to prioritize you. Not in a guilty, second-thought kind of way—but boldly, beautifully, and consistently.

> *"You can't pour from an empty cup. Take care of yourself first."*
> *— Unknown*

We often believe that self-care is selfish. That resting means we're lazy. That putting ourselves first means we're neglecting others. But what if the opposite is true?

What if the best way to love others... is to start by loving yourself well?

THE BURNOUT CYCLE

Here's how it usually goes: you give and give, until you're running on fumes. You smile through the exhaustion. You tell yourself, "I just have to push through." And when your body starts to shut down or your emotions spill over—you feel guilty for needing a break.

Sound familiar?

You are not a machine. You are a human being. And your needs matter.

I had a season where I was everything for everyone. Saying yes to every favor, every invitation, every text that needed a response. I wore exhaustion like a badge of honor. Until one day, I crashed—hard. Not just physically, but emotionally. My body said, "No more," because I hadn't been saying it myself.

RECLAIMING THE WORD 'SELFISH'

Let's redefine what it means to be "selfish."

Selfish isn't neglecting others—it's nurturing yourself so you can show up fully for others. It's taking time to refill your spirit, so you don't show up bitter, drained, or resentful.

> *"Almost everything will work again if you unplug it for a few minutes... including you."*
> — Anne Lamott

Practical Ways to Pour into Yourself

- Say no without apology. Your time is precious. Protect it.
- Create sacred space daily. Even if it's 10 minutes. Breathe. Stretch. Reflect.
- Do something that brings you joy. Just because. No productivity attached.
- Ask for help. You're not weak for needing support—you're wise.
- Celebrate yourself. Out loud. Regularly.

A Personal Becoming Moment: Refill

There was a morning I woke up and felt... empty. Not the kind of empty you feel after a bad night's sleep, but the deep, soul-level exhaustion that says, *You've been giving and giving and haven't stopped to refill.*

Nothing specific had happened the night before. No fight. No bad news. But my spirit felt drained, and my mind felt cluttered. For years, my default would've been to push through—show up for everyone else before even checking in on myself. But this time? I didn't.

I decided that before I poured into *anyone*, I was going to pour into me.

I lit my favorite candle—the one that smells like vanilla and warm spice—letting its glow and scent fill the air like a gentle reminder that I deserve comfort, too. I put on music that didn't demand anything from me, just soothed and wrapped around me like a soft blanket.

Then I sat with my journal, hands still, pen hovering above the page. At first, nothing came. Then the words started spilling out—frustrations, gratitude, prayers, dreams—everything I had been holding inside while tending to everyone else's needs. And the tears came, too. They weren't from weakness, but from release.

I prayed. I asked God to refill me—not just so I could keep going, but so I could keep *giving* without resentment, without depletion, without losing myself in the process.

By the time I closed my journal, something in me had shifted. I didn't feel "full" yet, but I felt steadier. I could breathe deeper. And when I finally walked into my day, I realized the truth:

You can't keep pouring from an empty cup and expect the water to be sweet.

It doesn't always take a full retreat or a week away. Sometimes, it just takes one intentional choice—to pour into yourself first—before you pour into the world.

Because the best version of you is the one that's filled, not running on fumes.

A Prayer for Refill and Restoration

Dear God,

I've given so much of myself to others, and I thank You for the heart You gave me to love.

But today, I come to You needing rest. Restoration. A refill.

Help me to release the guilt of putting myself first. Teach me to listen to what my mind, body, and spirit need.

Remind me that I am worthy of the same care and compassion I give so freely to others.

Let Your peace cover me. Let Your love fill me. Let Your presence refresh every part of me.

Amen.

Reflection Prompt:

Where in your life have you been overextending? What do you need more of?

Journaling Space:

Write a self-care menu. List five things that fill your cup and commit to doing at least one this week.

Affirmation

I am worthy of the time, space, and love I give to others. I choose to pour into myself first.

Chapter 11
Communication Isn't a Cuss Word-*K-LA*

Let's talk about it—literally.

And no, this isn't the part where I tell you to use your "I feel" statements while someone rolls their eyes, and you spiral into a mental episode of 'Why did I even try?' Communication gets a bad rap, but it's not the villain—it's just misunderstood. Like kale, but less crunchy.

For so many of us, communication has been wrapped in tension. We've been silenced, shut down, misunderstood, or dismissed. So now, instead of speaking, we suppress. Instead of sharing, we shut off. And instead of setting boundaries, we build walls.

But communication isn't the enemy—it's the *bridge*. It's the connection point between who you are and how others experience you.

"The biggest communication problem is that we do not listen to understand. We listen to reply." — Stephen R. Covey

You can't build healthy relationships without honest communication. That includes romantic, platonic, professional, and especially the one you have with yourself.

Why We Stay Silent

We stay silent because we're afraid. Afraid of being misunderstood. Afraid of being too much. Afraid of causing conflict. Afraid of not knowing what to say.

However, silence doesn't always maintain peace. Sometimes, it keeps you in pain.

There's power in naming your needs. In expressing your feelings. In speaking your truth with clarity and compassion.

A Personal Becoming Moment: Speak Up

There was a conversation I avoided for months. I told myself I didn't want to rock the boat. I didn't want to seem "dramatic" or "too much." I convinced myself that keeping quiet would keep the peace.

But here's the thing—silence doesn't keep peace; it just builds tension. And the more I held it in, the heavier it got.

At the time, I was getting to know someone I was interested in. You know that exciting stage where everything feels fresh and full of potential? Well… that honeymoon phase didn't last long. There were things that started to bother me—little inconsistencies, lack of communication, and this assumption on his part that somehow, effort was optional when it came to keeping my interest.

At first, I brushed it off. "It's no big deal." "Maybe he's just busy." "Don't make it a thing." But deep down, I knew it *was* a thing. It mattered. And every time I swallowed my feelings instead of expressing them, the weight of unspoken words grew heavier.

Finally, I couldn't take it anymore. I asked for a meeting—not a casual "let's talk," but a *real* sit-down. My voice trembled, my palms were sweaty, my stomach was in knots. But I spoke my truth—calmly, clearly, and without apology.

I told him what I had observed. I addressed the inconsistencies. I expressed my need for open, honest communication. I made it clear that effort was not just appreciated—it was necessary.

And guess what? The world didn't end. The relationship didn't instantly fall apart. In fact... it got better. Because clarity invites connection. My honesty gave us a chance to actually address the gaps instead of pretending they didn't exist.

That moment reminded me: discomfort is temporary, but regret lasts much longer. And I refuse to live in regret.

Sometimes the distraction isn't scrolling social media or watching one more episode of a show you've seen ten times—it's the avoidance of the conversations that could actually set you free.

HEALTHY COMMUNICATION LOOKS LIKE:

- **Speaking truthfully.** Even when it's hard.
- **Listening to understand.** Not just to respond.
- **Setting boundaries.** Clearly, kindly, firmly.
- **Using "I" statements.** Own your feelings and avoid blame.
- **Allowing space.** Not every conversation needs to be immediate or perfect.

How to Practice Brave Communication

1. **Start with self-awareness.** What do I really feel? What do I need?
2. **Choose the right time.** Timing matters. So does tone.
3. **Be clear, not cruel.** Honesty and kindness can coexist.
4. **Detach from outcomes.** You're responsible for your delivery, not their reaction.

"Speak your mind, even if your voice shakes."
—*Maggie Kuhn*

A Prayer for Courageous Communication

Dear God,

Thank You for giving me a voice. Help me use it with wisdom and grace.

Give me the courage to speak truthfully, the patience to listen deeply, and the humility to grow through every conversation.

Let my words be rooted in love and guided by clarity. And when I'm afraid, remind me that my voice matters.

Amen.

Reflection Prompt:

What conversation have you been avoiding, and why? What truth are you ready to express?

Journaling Space:

Write out the first few lines of a hard conversation you need to have. Let it be messy, but honest.

Affirmation

I communicate with clarity, compassion, and confidence. My voice is powerful, and my truth is worthy of expression.

Chapter 12
Distraction: How to Avoid It and Stay Focused

Welcome to Chapter 12—aka, the callout chapter.

This chapter might sting a little—but in a good way. Think of it like tough love with a side of snacks and a really good playlist to get you back on track. If you've ever opened your fridge five times in an hour just to avoid a task… this one's for you.

Don't worry, we're all in this together. If you've ever sat down to be productive and somehow ended up deep in a rabbit hole of cat videos, home DIYs you'll never do, or analyzing a stranger's vacation photos from 2017—welcome. You're human.

Distraction is the thief of progress. It wears many disguises: busyness, procrastination, even productivity that's not really purposeful. And it's sneaky because sometimes distraction *feels* like you're doing something important. But deep down, you know you're just avoiding the real work.

> *"You will never reach your destination if you stop and throw stones at every dog that barks."*
> — Winston Churchill

This chapter is about calling distraction out, taking your focus back, and creating a life that aligns with your goals and your growth.

THE REAL COST OF DISTRACTION

Distraction doesn't just delay you. It *derails* you. It pulls your energy, your attention, and your momentum away from what truly matters.

Think about it: how many times have you told yourself, "I'll start tomorrow"? And how many tomorrows have come and gone?

It's not about guilt—it's about awareness. Because when you know what's stealing your focus, you can take your power back.

Common Distractions and How to Handle Them

1. **Social Media Scroll-Holes**
   - Tip: Set time limits. Use app blockers. Replace one scroll session with a five-minute journal session.
2. **Overcommitting**
   - Tip: Say no. Full sentence. Protect your "yes" like your peace depends on it—because it does.
3. **Perfectionism**
   - Tip: Done is better than perfect. Progress is better than pretending.
4. **Emotional Avoidance**
   - Tip: Feel it to heal it. Sometimes we distract ourselves because we don't want to feel. Sit with the emotion. It's just passing through.

Let's take a deeper look at emotional avoidance—because this one's sneaky. When life feels heavy or uncertain, we often reach for something to *numb* rather than *nurture*.

It might be endless scrolling, binge-watching, overworking, or keeping busy just to avoid stillness. But here's the truth:

emotions aren't meant to be avoided. They're messengers. Signals. Invitations to go inward.

When I finally sat with my emotions—really sat with them—I realized how much I had been carrying. And once I acknowledged them, something powerful happened: they began to loosen their grip. Naming the feeling is the first step toward healing it.

So ask yourself: What am I *really* feeling right now? Where is this coming from? What do I need in this moment?

You don't have to fix it all. You just have to feel it and face it.

"Your emotions will not kill you but avoiding them might kill your peace."

My Personal Wake-Up Call

I remember sitting at my desk, overwhelmed with a to-do list that could've doubled as a novella. Instead of tackling it, I reorganized my spice rack. Yes, my spice rack (those that know me know that I don't have that may spices to organize).

It wasn't about the spices—it was about the fear of facing something I didn't feel ready for. That's when I realized: distraction isn't always about laziness. Sometimes, it's a disguise for fear.

From that moment on, I made a rule: when I feel the urge to do something that's "urgent but irrelevant," I pause and ask myself, *"What am I avoiding right now?"* That one question changed everything.

> *"What you don't change, you choose."*
> —*Unknown*

A Personal Becoming Moment: When I Faced My Own Noise

I used to think I was just "busy." Always on the go, always doing something—emails, errands, cleaning things that didn't even need to be cleaned. I wore my productivity like a badge of honor. But underneath the hustle was something deeper: avoidance.

One weekend, I decided to unplug and spend time alone—no distractions. Just me, my thoughts, and a quiet space. It sounded peaceful… until it wasn't.

Within an hour, I felt restless. I started reaching for my phone out of habit. I thought about laundry, organizing drawers, anything. But instead, I sat still.

And that's when the tears came. Out of nowhere. Not because anything "bad" had happened but because I had been moving so fast, I hadn't noticed how heavy I felt inside. I was exhausted. Not just physically, but emotionally. I realized I had been using busyness to avoid stillness, because stillness required me to listen—to myself.

That day changed me. I learned that silence isn't empty it's full of answers. And now, whenever I feel myself reaching for distraction, I pause and ask: *What truth am I running from?* It always leads me back to what matters.

Reclaiming Your Focus

- **Start your day with intention** – Don't let your phone be the first voice you hear. Ground yourself before the world gets access to you.
- **Create a distraction-free zone** – No, you don't need a perfect office. Just a corner with clarity.
- **Schedule your priorities** – If it matters, it deserves time on your calendar.
- **Take breaks** – Your brain needs breathing room. Just make sure breaks don't turn into detours.

And remember focus isn't about doing more. It's about doing what matters.

A Prayer for Clarity and Presence

Dear God,

I come to You distracted and pulled in a thousand directions.

Quiet the noise around me and within me. Help me release what doesn't matter and anchor myself in what does.

Give me the courage to face the feelings I've been avoiding and the wisdom to hear what they're trying to tell me.

Teach me to focus, not just on tasks, but on truth. On purpose. On presence.

Thank You for being my constant in the chaos. Walk with me as I choose presence over pressure and peace over panic.

Amen.

Reflection Prompt:

What distractions show up most often in your life? What are they possibly protecting you from facing?

Journaling Space:

Create a "Focus Game Plan." List 3 things you can do this week to reduce distractions and protect your attention.

Affirmation

I choose to focus over fear. I am present, powerful, and committed to what matters most.

Chapter 13

Protecting Your Peace

Some days it feels like peace is an endangered species and your phone is a walking chaos portal.

Whether it's toxic group chats, workplace drama, overcommitted calendars, or your own overthinking—protecting your peace in today's world is nothing short of a spiritual practice. But let me remind you: your peace is not a luxury. It's a necessity.

> *"Peace is not the absence of chaos,*
> *but the presence of clarity."*
> *—Unknown*

This chapter is about building internal and external boundaries that guard your well-being, protect your energy, and honor your healing. Because you weren't made to constantly live in survival mode. You were made to thrive.

Why Peace Feels So Hard to Maintain

Let's face it peace often feels like something we have to earn after the work is done, the inbox is cleared, and the people are pleased. But peace isn't a finish line. It's a practice. And it's available to you right now.

Peace is hard to hold when:

- You don't feel safe to rest.
- You're addicted to productivity.
- You're afraid people will think you've changed.
- You feel guilty for doing less or needing more.

But hear me: protecting your peace isn't about cutting everyone off and moving to a cabin in the woods (though that does sound nice some days). It's about making choices every day that align with your values, protect your energy, and keep you centered.

One big peace thief? People-pleasing.

We bend, twist, stretch, and contort ourselves to keep everyone else comfortable—until we've got no comfort left for ourselves. Protecting your peace means you stop over-functioning for others at the expense of your own emotional, spiritual, and physical well-being.

> *"You can be a good person with a kind heart and still say no."*
> —Lori Deschene

Signs Your Peace Is Under Attack

- You wake up feeling anxious before the day begins.
- You're constantly people-pleasing, even when it hurts.
- You feel the need to explain or defend your boundaries.
- Your body is tired, but your brain won't stop spinning.
- You can't remember the last time you felt calm on the inside.
- You dread quiet moments because your mind becomes too loud.
- You're starting to resent people you used to enjoy—because you've been giving from an empty cup.

If any of these feel familiar, your peace has been compromised—and it's time to take it back.

A Personal Becoming Moment: When I Said No to Chaos

There was a season where everything looked great on the outside but on the inside? I was overwhelmed, snappy, and emotionally exhausted. I said yes to things I didn't want to do. I kept silent in places I should've spoken up. I let other people's drama become my daily diet.

One day, I took my peace back.

I muted conversations. I canceled an event that felt forced. I took a slow walk. I breathed. I journaled. I remembered who I was. And you know what? Nothing exploded. Nobody died. The world went on.

And I felt lighter.

That was the moment I decided that peace was not something I'd find by accident. It was something I had to protect on purpose.

That wasn't a one-time thing. Since then, I've had to keep choosing peace even when it made me look selfish, different, or "unavailable."

But here's the truth: peace isn't passive. It's powerful.

PROTECTING YOUR PEACE IN REAL LIFE

- Create boundaries—and stick to them. You don't need to explain.
- Mute the noise. Yes, that includes your phone.
- Declutter your calendar. Just because it fits doesn't mean it belongs.
- Make rest non-negotiable. Rest is productive.
- Let people be disappointed. Their reaction isn't your responsibility.
- Spend time alone. Stillness is where peace is born.
- Start your day in silence. Before the world talks at you, listen to your own soul.
- Be okay with missing out. FOMO fades—peace stays.

> *"The more peaceful you become, the less you tolerate anything that disturbs it."*
> —Sylvester McNutt

PEACE VS. PERFORMANCE

We live in a world that glorifies hustle, grind, and being "on" all the time. But at what cost?

You weren't created to perform 24/7. You were created to live. To breathe. To enjoy. To experience joy without guilt. To rest without apology.

If you're constantly performing for approval, you'll never feel at peace—because performance is about control, and peace is about surrender.

When you finally let go of needing to prove, impress, or perfect, you free yourself to rest in who you already are.

What Protecting Peace Really Means

It means letting go of what's loud but not loving. What's urgent but not important. What's familiar but not fruitful.

It means choosing silence over shouting. Grace over guilt. Presence over pressure.

Peace isn't always pretty. Sometimes it looks like walking away. Turning off your phone. Saying no. Going to bed early. Leaving the conversation. Choosing quiet strength over loud reaction.

But every time you choose peace, you choose you.

Protecting Peace at Home

Your home should feel like a sanctuary—not a source of stress. Protect your peace at home by:

- Creating cozy, calm spaces with soft lighting and music.
- Having family meetings to reset expectations and communication.
- Making sacred rituals—tea, journaling, prayer, silence.
- Decluttering physical space to reflect inner clarity.
- Saying, "I need space," without guilt.

Peace doesn't just happen—it's designed.

PROTECTING PEACE IN RELATIONSHIPS

This part is tough. But vital.

Some people simply don't know how to interact without chaos. Protecting your peace might mean limiting time with certain friends, keeping topics off-limits, or even ending connections that continually drain you.

Love doesn't mean unlimited access. You can love people and still guard your spirit.

A Prayer for Peace That Lasts

Dear God,

Thank You for being my anchor in the storm. Help me to guard my heart, calm my mind, and protect my peace with boldness and grace.

Teach me to say no without guilt, to rest without shame, and to be still without fear.

Let my life reflect the peace I've prayed for. And when the world tries to shake me, remind me that You are my center.

Let Your peace flow through every decision, every boundary, and every moment of stillness.

Amen.

Reflection Prompt:

Where in your life is your peace being threatened? What boundary or change can you make this week to protect it?

Bonus Prompt:

What would it look like to create a daily peace ritual just for you?

Journaling Space:

Make a "Peace Plan." List five things that restore your peace—and commit to doing at least one daily.

Affirmation

Peace is my power. I protect it fiercely, honor it daily, and carry it with me everywhere I go.

Chapter 14
Unlearning Desperation

Desperation is not cute! You can put on the best outfit, do the hair, the nails, the makeup, and walk in smelling like you just bathed in "Confidence No. 5," but if your energy is screaming *"Please pick me!"*, people will smell it before they even hug you. Desperation has a way of clinging to your aura like bad cologne — strong, overwhelming, and hard to ignore.

And I can say that with confidence because there was a time I was practically bathing in it. If desperation had a rewards program, I'd have been a platinum member with exclusive access to the "Over-Give & Under-Receive" lounge. Complimentary snacks? Of course — provided by me, because I was always the one bringing the most to the table and leaving the hungriest.

CALLING IT WHAT IT IS

We like to disguise desperation with prettier words: "I'm just loyal," "I'm just invested," "I'm just supportive." No sis… you're just scared. Scared to lose them. Scared to be alone. Scared they'll realize you're not perfect (spoiler alert: you're not, and neither are they).

The truth is, desperation makes us audition for roles in people's lives they never even posted a casting call for. You keep reading lines, hoping to get the part, when they're not even looking for an actress.

How It Shows Up

- You agree to things you don't want to do because you're afraid saying no will push them away.

- You over-give to people who never meet you halfway.
- You tolerate disrespect, waiting for the "good side" of them to return.
- You measure your worth by how much someone else notices or appreciates you.

A PERSONAL BECOMING MOMENT: BREAKTHROUGH

One of my clearest "wake up" moments happened on a Sunday afternoon in — you guessed it — my car. Seems my car is my personal therapy office without the copay.

I had just finished running around for someone who swore they "needed me." I skipped my own plans, spent my own gas, rearranged my own day — and when I dropped off what they needed, they barely said thank you. No hug, no eye contact, just a casual "Cool, thanks" before disappearing back into their world.

I sat there in my car, staring at the steering wheel, and this thought hit me like it was sent straight from heaven: *"Tanya, you are doing too much... for too little."*

And I had to laugh — not because it was funny, but because it was embarrassingly true.

That day, I decided I was done hustling for scraps of affection, validation, or approval. I was done "performing" for love like it was open-mic night and the audience was stingy with applause. The right people would never require me to lose myself to keep them. The wrong ones would fall away when I stopped overcompensating — and that was fine.

The Process of Unlearning

Unlearning desperation is a daily choice.

- **Pause before reacting.** If you feel the urge to over-give, ask yourself: *Is this from love, or fear?*
- **Detach your worth from their response.** You are valuable whether they see it or not.
- **Learn to sit in the silence.** Sometimes not chasing is the most powerful move you can make.

The Courage to Let Go

When you stop clinging, you'll realize some people never had a real hold on you — they just had a hold on your fear. Once you cut that cord, you'll see the relationships that remain are the ones built on choice, not obligation.

Prayer for Freedom from Desperation

God, help me to love myself so fully that I never feel the need to beg for love from others.

Teach me to release what is not meant for me and to trust that You will fill every empty space with peace, not panic.

May my spirit be rooted in worth, and may my heart beat in rhythm with Your truth.

Amen

Reflection Prompt

Think about a recent time when you said "yes" out of fear of losing someone's approval.

- What did that cost you emotionally or physically?
- If you had said "no," how might things have been different?
- What would it look like to respond from a place of self-worth next time?

Journaling Space:

Affirmation

I no longer audition for roles in anyone's life.

I am chosen, valued, and loved without performing.

The right people will stay because of who I am, not what I can do for them.

Part IV

ALIGNMENT & EMBODIMENT

Chapter 15
Redefining Success

Let's start with this: if success still looks like someone else's Instagram highlight reel, we've got some unlearning to do.

Seriously. For years, I thought success meant hustling nonstop, checking all the boxes, and smiling through burnout like it was some kind of achievement badge. But somewhere along the way, I realized: I was living for applause that didn't even feed me.

"Success is liking yourself, liking what you do, and liking how you do it." — Maya Angelou

This chapter is about reclaiming your definition of success—based on your *values*, your *joy*, and your *well-being*, not someone else's version of "making it."

Why We Need a New Definition

The old model of success is loud, exhausting, and external:

- A certain income.
- A perfect body.
- A packed calendar.
- A curated life.

But here's the truth: you can have all of that and still feel hollow inside.

Real success isn't about how busy you are. It's about how *whole* you are.

It's about:

- Waking up with peace.
- Doing work that feels purposeful.
- Loving your life even when it's quiet.
- Being able to rest without guilt.

Redefining success means trading hustle for harmony, status for soul, and pressure for presence.

The Sneaky Pressure to Perform

Success has often been wrapped up in approval. We start chasing gold stars from a young age. Be the best student. The best daughter. The most liked. The most responsible. And that need to perform follows us into adulthood like a clingy sidekick.

You end up living on autopilot, following paths that look successful on the outside but feel misaligned on the inside. You hit goals that should feel good—but don't. You get what you thought you wanted and still feel empty.

That's how you know it's time to redefine success.

"When you stop living for applause, you start living for purpose."

A Personal Shift

There was a time when I measured my worth by how much I got done in a day. If I didn't check everything off my list, I felt like I failed. My joy was buried under a mountain of unrealistic expectations.

Then one day, I asked myself, "What if success isn't about doing more—but about *being more* present, peaceful, and aligned?"

So, I started measuring success by how often I laughed. By how rested I felt. By how connected I was to my purpose.

And you know what? I got more done—with more joy, less stress, and a whole lot more soul.

It was no longer about how many things I accomplished—but how aligned I felt while doing them.

WHAT DOES SUCCESS MEAN TO YOU?

Let's take back the narrative. Try finishing these prompts:

- Success looks like...
- Success feels like...
- I feel most successful when...
- I know I'm aligned with my purpose when...

These are the real markers. Not titles, not followers, not paychecks—but *peace, presence, and purpose.*

> *"Don't confuse having a career with having a life."*
> —Hillary Clinton

Your success may be having a calm morning routine. Or walking away from what no longer serves you. Or creating a life where you don't need a vacation to escape.

RED FLAGS YOU'RE LIVING SOMEONE ELSE'S VERSION OF SUCCESS

- You constantly compare your life to others.
- You achieve goals but still feel empty.
- You fear slowing down will make you irrelevant.
- You measure your value by your productivity.
- You're doing what looks good instead of what feels right.
- You're exhausted and don't know why.
- You dread the life you're working so hard to maintain.

If any of this sounds familiar, pause. Breathe. Realign. Your path doesn't have to look like theirs to be meaningful.

REDEFINING SUCCESS PRACTICALLY

1. **Write your own definition.** Make it personal. Make it powerful.
2. **Create success metrics that matter.** Example: joy level, impact, rest, connection.
3. **Audit your current goals.** Are they truly *yours*?
4. **Release the timelines.** There is no deadline on becoming.
5. **Celebrate progress—not perfection.** Growth is still success.
6. **Stop asking, "What should I be doing?" and start asking, "What do I want to feel?"**

Success that's aligned with your truth will never require you to abandon yourself to get it.

When Slowing Down IS Success

In a world obsessed with hustle, resting becomes a radical act. Choosing peace over pressure. Choosing joy over performance.

Some of the most successful seasons of my life have looked like:

- Saying no without guilt.
- Going to therapy.
- Spending more time with loved ones.
- Creating margin in my day for breathing, thinking, and dreaming.

Success can look like peace. Success can feel like balance. Success can sound like laughter. Success can be soft, quiet, and sacred.

The Inner Success Inventory

Try this: make a list of things that make you feel most like yourself. Then ask:

- How often am I doing these things?
- What's getting in the way?
- How can I build my life around *this*?

This list is your internal compass. When life gets loud, come back to this.

A Prayer for Alignment and Purpose

Dear God,

Thank You for reminding me that I was not created to chase—but to live, to love, and to serve with intention.

Help me release the pressure to prove and embrace the peace of being present.

Let my success be measured by alignment, not approval. By joy, not just achievement.

Keep me rooted in what matters. Remind me that I am enough—even now.

Show me how to build a life that reflects my soul—not just my schedule.

Amen.

Reflection Prompt:

What definition of success have you been living by? Is it time to rewrite it?

Bonus Prompt:

What does *soul-aligned* success look and feel like for you? How can you bring more of that into your daily life?

Journaling Space:

Create your new definition of success. Let it be rooted in who you truly are—not who you think you're supposed to be.

Write it on a post-it. Tape it to your mirror. Let it guide your next move.

Affirmation

Success is being fully, freely, and unapologetically myself. I am already enough. I define my path—and it is beautiful.

My success honors my truth, my joy, and my journey.

Chapter 16
Achieving the Goals, Dreams, and Aspirations You Desire

First things first: you've made it to Chapter 16—look at you go!

You didn't just survive the emotional deep dives—you made it to the action chapter! Cue the confetti and caffeine. This is where we trade the tissue box for a vision board (but keep the snacks nearby, just in case).

Seriously, pause for a second and give yourself a moment of recognition. You've been doing the work—unpacking, unlearning, unlocking—and now we're stepping into the part that's going to take all that internal growth and turn it into external action.

This is the part where we talk about dreams—not the fluffy kind you scribbled on a vision board and forgot about. I'm talking about the soul-deep, can't-let-it-go, wake-you-up-at-2AM kind of dreams. The goals you secretly whisper to yourself when no one's listening. The ones that scare you a little... and excite you a lot.

> *"Go confidently in the direction of your dreams. Live the life you have imagined."*
> — *Henry David Thoreau*

Let's be real—dream-chasing isn't always glamorous. It's not just posting motivational quotes and writing to-do lists in cute planners. It's grit. It's discipline. It's saying no to distractions and yes to discomfort. It's failing forward and celebrating small wins. It's showing up when no one's clapping.

And most importantly it's believing you are *worthy* of what you want.

GETTING CLEAR ON WHAT YOU REALLY WANT

Let's start here: what do you *really* want?

Not what looks good on social media. Not what your family or friends think you should want. Not what you settled for because it felt safer.

What do *you* want? What lights your soul on fire?

Write it down. Say it out loud. Let it breathe.

One of my own turning points came when I finally admitted a dream I'd buried for years. I wanted to write a book. I had every excuse in the world—I wasn't ready, I wasn't qualified, who would read it? But deep down, I *knew*. That dream wouldn't leave me alone because it was mine to fulfill.

Clarity is the first step. You can't chase what you won't claim.

FACING THE FEAR

Once you get clear, the fear will try to creep in. That's normal. But fear doesn't get to drive.

You'll hear voices—some internal, some external—saying:

- "What if you fail?"
- "What if you're not good enough?"
- "Who do you think you are?"

Here's how you answer: *"I am becoming her. Watch me."*

"Feel the fear and do it anyway." — Susan Jeffers

Fear is not your enemy. It's just a sign that you're doing something meaningful. Let it walk beside you—but don't hand it the map.

Making a Plan and Taking Action

Dreams need structure. Passion needs a plan.

Break your big goals into small steps. Tiny, manageable, realistic steps. Every single day, do *one thing* that moves you closer. It could be writing a paragraph, sending an email, doing research, or even taking a break to recharge.

Progress isn't about speed it's about consistency.

Let me share something close to my heart: one of my personal goals was to start a foundation in honor of my son. It wasn't just a dream—it was a calling. But at first, the idea felt too big. Too emotional. Too heavy.

There were days I doubted myself, questioned my strength, wondered if anyone would care. But the dream kept tugging. So I started with one small step—brainstorming names. Then I made a mission statement. Then I had a conversation with someone who believed in the vision.

And now? That dream is living, breathing, impacting lives. It's not about doing it all at once. It's about doing one thing at a time—with purpose, with love, with heart.

So don't underestimate your steps, no matter how small they feel. Your dream deserves your faith.

And celebrate every single win. You got up early? Win. You made a scary phone call? Win. You rested instead of burning out? Also a win.

A Personal Becoming Moment:

Grief can be a thief—it steals your joy, your energy, and sometimes even your sense of direction. When my son passed, the world as I knew it crumbled. The days felt long but the nights felt longer, and I was living in this haze of pain and disbelief. There was this aching inside me, this need to do *something* to honor him, but I didn't know where to start.

One day, the thought came to me: *What if I created something in his name?* I imagined a foundation focused on motorcycle safety—a cause close to my heart and his. I pictured providing motorcycle equipment to those who needed it, hosting fundraisers, and creating events to spread awareness about safety on the road.

And then… the other voice came.

That shadowy, doubting whisper that creeps in just when you start to dream.

"Why would you do that? It's too big. You don't have the resources. It won't work. You can't make that happen."

For a moment, I almost believed it. Almost. But something inside me—something stronger—rose up and said, *No. This matters. He matters. And I'm going to do it anyway.*

So, I ignored that voice of fear and moved forward. Step by step. Conversation by conversation. And today, what was once just an idea is a living, breathing reality: The ANT777 Motorcycle Foundation.

This foundation isn't just a tribute—it's a movement. It's a way to protect other riders, to raise awareness, and to keep my son's name alive in a way that saves lives. And every time I see someone wearing the gear we've provided, every time we host a fundraiser, every time someone tells me they're more mindful on the road because of our work—I know I stepped into the light, not just for him, but for myself.

I could have stayed in the shadows of grief. But I chose to stand in the sunlight of purpose.

> *"A dream written down with a date becomes a goal. A goal broken down into steps becomes a plan. A plan backed by action becomes reality."*
> —Greg Reid

A Prayer for Purpose and Progress

Dear God,

Thank You for the dreams You've placed in my heart. Even when they feel far away, remind me that You planted them there for a reason.

Give me the strength to take bold steps and the patience to wait with grace. Help me to believe in myself the way You believe in me.

Let my actions be led by faith, not fear. Let my passion be bigger than my doubt.

And even when the journey feels slow, help me trust that You are working behind the scenes.

I commit my goals, my plans, and my purpose to You. Walk with me every step of the way.

Amen.

Reflection Prompt:

What goal or dream have you been putting off? What's one step you can take today to move toward it?

Journaling Space:

Write out a mini-action plan. Three small steps. One big intention.

Affirmation

I am capable, equipped, and ready to walk boldly in the direction of my dreams.

Chapter 17
Come Out of the Shadows and Into the Light

Welcome back, you resilient, radiant soul.

If you've made it this far without tossing the book across the room or dramatically whispering "Whew, this is too real," then congratulations—you're officially a survivor of some deep inner work. Go ahead, adjust your crown. You've earned it.

If you're still here reading, that means you're serious about this becoming journey. And I want you to know—I see you. I see the parts of you that are healing, that are learning to love again, that are tired but still trying. That takes *real* strength.

Now let's get into something deep... but necessary.

Because if we're being real, most of us don't just *live* in the shadows—we've *survived* in them. Hidden in them. Made homes in them. We've dimmed ourselves so others wouldn't feel uncomfortable. We've silenced our gifts, our power, our truth... and for what?

To be accepted? To avoid judgment? To not make waves?

"You were not born to shrink. You were born to shine."

This chapter is about *owning all of who you are*—even the messy, misunderstood, and magical parts—and boldly stepping into your light.

Why We Hide

Let's go ahead and say it: hiding feels safe. It's warm. It's predictable. No one can reject the version of you they never get to fully see. But at what cost?

Every time you hold back your truth, you chip away at your authenticity. Every time you say "I'm fine" when you're breaking inside, you create a divide between who you are and who you pretend to be.

I used to be the queen of pretending. Smiling when I wanted to cry. Nodding in agreement when everything in me wanted to scream, "This isn't okay." I didn't want to seem weak. I didn't want to be too much. I didn't want to be *judged*.

But guess what? The judgment came anyway. Because no matter how much you try to please people, someone's always going to have something to say.

> *"I'd rather be hated for who I am than loved for who I'm not."*
> — Kurt Cobain

So I started choosing truth. Slowly. Painfully. But truthfully.

Light Doesn't Mean Perfect

Here's what I had to learn: coming into the light doesn't mean you're flawless. It means you're *real*.

It means you walk in a room with your head held high *and* a past that tried to break you. It means you speak with boldness even if your voice trembles. It means you stop dimming your intelligence, your style, your story to make others comfortable.

Your light isn't for decoration it's for direction. Somebody out there needs what only *you* can bring.

THE MOMENT I STEPPED INTO THE LIGHT

It was during a conversation with a friend. I had been going through a rough season but hadn't told anyone. She asked, "How are you really?" And for the first time, I didn't sugarcoat it.

I said, "Honestly? I'm tired. I'm confused. I'm hurt. But I'm trying."

Her response? "Thank you. I needed to hear that. I thought I was the only one."

That was the moment I realized: my honesty gave her permission to be honest too. My light made space for hers. That's the power of authenticity. That's what happens when you come out of hiding.

A PERSONAL BECOMING MOMENT

Have you ever show up to an event thinking you're just there to eat snacks, sip something nice, and mind your business—only to have life snatch you right out of your comfort zone? Yeah… that was me.

I had been invited by a published author to attend her event. I thought I'd be in the audience, nodding my head, clapping at all the right moments, and maybe even slipping out early if I felt awkward. What I *didn't* know was that this event wasn't just about listening it was about sharing.

Here's the thing: I didn't tell my circle I was going. This was something I needed to do alone. I wanted to push myself, meet new people, and stretch beyond the comfortable little box I had built for myself.

Then… it happened. My name was called.

I could feel my heart drop into my shoes. My first instinct was to smile politely and decline. The fear in my chest was loud and convincing. But then—clear as day—I heard the Spirit whisper: *"Share."*

And so, I got up. My hands were shaking, but I pulled out my poem, *Beautifully Crafted*—something deeply personal, something that felt like a piece of my soul wrapped in words.

I read it aloud for the very first time. When I finished, there was silence. For a second, I thought, *"Welp, that's it. I've just embarrassed myself in front of a room full of strangers."*

Then… the applause came. And it wasn't polite, halfway clapping—it was full, warm, genuine. That moment shifted something in me.

I realized that sometimes the thing you're most afraid of doing is the very thing that unlocks the next version of yourself. That night, I didn't just read a poem—I stepped into my voice. I met the woman I was becoming. And I am forever grateful for that moment.

THE COST OF DIMMING

Every time you dim your light to make someone else feel comfortable, you abandon a piece of your purpose.

You were not designed to be a background character in your own life. You are the main character. And it's time to show up like it.

Does that mean it won't be uncomfortable? No. It means it will be *worth it*.

> *"If you avoid conflict to keep the peace,*
> *you start a war within yourself."*
> *— Cheryl Richardson*

STEPPING BOLDLY INTO THE LIGHT

Start small. Tell your truth to someone safe. Wear the outfit you love but were too afraid to rock. Say "no" when you mean it. Say "yes" when it scares you—in a good way.

Coming into the light is a practice. And every day you show up as yourself is a win.

A Prayer for Courage

Dear God,

Give me the courage to stop hiding the pieces of me that are sacred, true, and full of purpose.

When fear whispers that I'm too much or not enough, help me remember I am made in Your image—bold, brilliant, and whole.

Let me speak truth even when my voice trembles. Let me show up fully, even when I feel vulnerable.

Surround me with reminders that my light is needed in this world. And when I'm tempted to shrink, remind me that shrinking serves no one.

I trust You to walk with me as I rise.

Amen.

Remember: You don't owe the world a perfect version of you. But you do owe yourself the freedom to be fully seen.

Reflection Prompt:

Where in your life have you been hiding? What part of you is ready to be seen, heard, and celebrated?

Journaling Space:

Write a declaration: "I am stepping into the light because…" and finish the sentence with truth and boldness.

Affirmation

I will no longer hide who I am. My light is sacred, powerful, and meant to be seen.

Chapter 18
Be That Before You Expect It-K-LA

Let's get one thing straight: you don't attract what you want. You attract what you are.

And before you roll your eyes at another cliché Instagram quote, hear me out.

You can make the vision board. You can say the affirmations. You can light the candles, set the intentions, and even "manifest like a mogul." But if your daily thoughts, habits, relationships, and mindset don't match the frequency of what you say you desire? Then what you're really practicing is performance, not preparation.

- Expectation Without Alignment is Just Fantasy.
- We expect loyalty but don't know how to be loyal to ourselves.
- We expect peace but feed on drama.
- We expect deep love while still tolerating shallow connections.
- We expect miracles… but rarely prepare to receive them.

> *"Don't wait for the life you want to show up. Become the woman who lives it, breathes it, and protects it."*
> — Mary Wollstonecraft

You Can't Call in What You Keep Canceling Out

This is a chapter about alignment. About embodiment.

About becoming the thing you're praying for—before it knocks on your door.

Because when you are the thing you want, it no longer feels foreign when it arrives. It feels familiar. It feels deserved.

Want love? Be love.

Want peace? Protect your peace like it's rent money.

Want abundance? Make choices like you're already abundant.

Want a strong partnership? Become the kind of partner you want to receive.

Want respect? Start by telling yourself the truth, even when it's uncomfortable.

The Work of Becoming

Being what you expect means:

- Living your own standards so they aren't just a wishlist — they're your reality.
- Practicing the energy you want to receive, even when no one's watching.
- Letting your actions speak louder than your requirements.

It's not about being "worthy enough" for love, friendship, or success — you already are. It's about making sure that when the good comes, it recognizes you as home.

A Personal Becoming Moment: The Mirror Moment

I learned this lesson the hard way through my best friend, Kendra "K-LA" Anderson. Kendra had a way of giving love that was so present, you never had to wonder if you mattered to her. She showed up — not just when it was easy, but when it was inconvenient, messy, and complicated. She didn't just expect loyalty, she embodied it.

I remember one day calling her, venting about someone in my life who wasn't showing up for me the way I wanted. Kendra listened — really listened — and then said, "Tanya, are you showing up for yourself that way?"

It stopped me cold.

Because the truth was… I wasn't. I was asking for consistency while I was canceling on my own goals. I was demanding honesty while still sugarcoating my truth to avoid conflict. I was expecting the royal treatment while giving myself leftovers.

That moment was my mirror check — and it changed the way I approached every relationship, starting with the one I had with myself.

A Prayer for Embodiment

God, help me close the gap between what I want and who I'm willing to be.

Let me not just dream about the life I desire—

Let me become the woman who walks in it.

Teach me to trust the process, honor the practice, and be unapologetic about my growth.

Make me a magnet for the things I'm ready to receive.

Amen.

Journal Prompts

- What's one area of your life where your words and actions are not in alignment?
- What are you expecting that you're not currently embodying?
- What would it look like if you became the woman who already has what you're asking for?

Affirmation

I am already becoming everything I desire.

I don't chase—I attract. I don't wait—I embody.

I am not available for less than alignment.

Chapter 19
Becoming Her—In Action

Cue the drumroll… because this is where we take everything we've unpacked, unlearned, healed, and affirmed—and turn it into LIVING.

Yes, sis. You didn't come this far just to nod your head and highlight quotes. This is the chapter where we move from inspiration to *implementation*. From theory to transformation.

> *"Don't just talk about the woman
> you're becoming. BE her."*
> — *Unknown*

You've read the words. You've done the journaling. You've cried, laughed, paused, and prayed. And now? You step forward—not perfectly, but powerfully.

This chapter is your blueprint. Your compass. Your action plan for becoming the woman you've always been, beneath the noise, the doubt, and the dust life tried to bury you under.

BECOMING HER IS A DAILY DECISION

The woman you're becoming? She doesn't show up by accident. She is built in the quiet choices. She is shaped in the small moments. She is called forward—in the way you speak to yourself, love yourself, honor yourself.

Becoming her isn't a one-time breakthrough. It's a commitment to keep showing up as your highest self—even when it's uncomfortable. Even when it's unpopular. Even when it's inconvenient.

"You won't always feel ready. But you can choose to be real."
— YOU, every time you dare to show up fully."

Some days she'll show up radiant. Some days she'll show up shaky. But she'll still show up—and that's what counts.

Your Becoming Checklist

Here are some bold, sacred, everyday things that help you embody your evolution:

- **Speak up even when your voice shakes.**
- **Rest without explaining yourself.**
- **Set boundaries that make you feel safe, not just liked.**
- **Walk away from chaos, even if it's familiar.**
- **Celebrate your wins—out loud.**
- **Ask for what you need. Clearly. Boldly.**
- **Show compassion to your past self.**
- **Choose your values over validation.**
- **Surround yourself with people who reflect your next level, not your last chapter.**

Becoming her means curating your space, your relationships, your thoughts—even your self-talk—to match the woman you're growing into.

A Personal Becoming Moment

There was a day I had to choose: the comfort of who I used to be—or the clarity of who I was becoming.

It wasn't a big, cinematic moment. It was quiet. Private. Painful. But also liberating.

I looked in the mirror and said, "We're done pretending. We're done shrinking. We're done waiting for permission."

That was the day I started dressing like the woman I admired. Talking to myself with love. Taking the first steps of a vision I'd been afraid to pursue.

I didn't become her overnight. But that day? I decided she was worth becoming.

I said no to opportunities that felt misaligned—even though they were tempting. I distanced myself from relationships that no longer honored my growth. I stopped apologizing for needing time, space, or silence.

And every little step pulled me closer to her.

BECOMING HER IS NOT LINEAR

Some days you'll feel like you're soaring. Other days, you'll question everything. That's normal.

Becoming her doesn't mean you never feel fear. It means you keep moving anyway.

You'll backslide sometimes. You'll make mistakes. You'll second guess. That's okay. Every journey has detours. But the key is to keep going. Keep returning. Keep aligning.

Give yourself grace for the in-between.

> *"Transformation is less about lightning strikes and more about gentle rain that soaks the roots."*
> —Unknown

YOUR DAILY BECOMING PRACTICE

Here's a simple framework you can return to every morning:

1. **Ask:** Who do I want to be today?
2. **Act:** What does that version of me do first?
3. **Align:** What would she say yes to? No to?
4. **Affirm:** Speak truth over yourself. Out loud.
5. **Adjust:** What needs to shift so I can support her?

She is not a fantasy. She is *you*—fully stepped into.

HABITS THAT SUPPORT HER

- **Morning rituals that ground you.** Start the day with your soul, not your screen.
- **Movement that energizes.** Not punishment—celebration.
- **Mental hygiene.** Journal. Meditate. Pray. Clear the clutter.
- **Protective boundaries.** Peace is part of your self-care.
- **Lifelong learning.** Read, listen, expand. The woman you're becoming is curious.

Reflection Prompt:

What does the highest, most authentic version of you look like? Sound like? Feel like? How can you practice *being* her, starting today?

Bonus Prompt:

What would your schedule look like if it reflected the woman you're becoming?

A Prayer for Courage and Commitment

Dear God,

Thank You for awakening the woman inside me who is bold, loving, whole, and rising.

Help me walk in her truth. Help me speak from her power. Help me love from her heart.

When fear whispers, remind me of who I am. When doubt lingers, show me who You created me to be.

I am not waiting to become her—I am already becoming. And I trust You to finish what You started in me.

Amen.

Journaling Space:

Write a "Becoming Her Manifesto." Let it be bold, beautiful, and deeply personal.

Affirmation

I am not becoming someone new—I am returning to the powerful, radiant, authentic woman I've always been.

I choose her. I honor her. I show up as her

Part 5

LEGACY & REFLECTION

Chapter 20
My Life Journey and the Lessons I've Learned

This is the part of the book where you deserve a trophy. You've made it through the emotional gym, lifted some heavy truths, and maybe even sweated through a few breakthroughs. This chapter isn't here to test you—it's here to celebrate you. And yes, snacks are still encouraged.

This chapter is a love letter to the woman I've been, the woman I am, and the woman I'm still becoming.

If you've made it this far, you already know—this isn't a straight-line journey. It's full of detours, setbacks, breakthroughs, and divine reroutes. And every single step, even the ones that felt like failure, has taught me something about strength, surrender, and self-worth.

> *"Life will keep teaching you the same lesson until you learn it."*
> *—Unknown*

This chapter is about the wisdom earned, the scars healed, and the grace received along the way. Maybe some of these lessons will feel familiar to you. Maybe you're still walking through some of them now. Either way, I hope you feel seen, supported, and reminded that you're never alone in your journey.

LESSON 1: YOU CAN BREAK AND STILL BLOOM.

I used to believe that being broken meant I was failing. But healing showed me that breaking is often the beginning of rebuilding. Some of my most powerful moments came after I thought I had nothing left. Your strength isn't in how well you avoid breaking—it's in how beautifully you rise after you do.

LESSON 2: GRIEF IS NOT A WEAKNESS. IT'S A FORM OF LOVE.

Losing my son changed me forever. There are no words big enough to hold that kind of ache. But through the grief, I learned to love harder, live fuller, and honor him by continuing to show up. Grief carved a deeper space in me—for compassion, perspective, and purpose.

LESSON 3: FORGIVENESS IS FREEDOM.

Forgiveness isn't about excusing the hurt. It's about releasing *yourself* from it. I've had to forgive others, yes—but even more, I've had to forgive *me*. For the things I didn't know. The mistakes I made. The ways I abandoned myself trying to please others. That forgiveness brought peace I didn't know I needed.

> *"Forgiveness is giving up the hope that the past could have been any different."*
> —Oprah Winfrey

LESSON 4: GOD'S TIMING > MY TIMELINE.

Whew, this one. I've tried to rush healing. Force doors open. Make things happen because I didn't want to wait. But time and time again, I've been reminded: what's meant for me won't miss me. Delay doesn't mean denial. Sometimes it's protection.

Lesson 5: I am enough—even when I'm evolving.

The woman I used to be needed outside validation to feel worthy. The woman I'm becoming knows she carries worth with every breath. I've learned that self-love is not a destination. It's a daily decision to honor my voice, my body, my truth.

A Moment of Reflection

There's something sacred about looking back and seeing how far you've come. The tears you cried, the nights you prayed, the courage it took to keep going—all of it matters. All of it shaped you.

You didn't just survive—you *became*.

So take a breath. Put your hand over your heart. Whisper thank you—to the version of you that got you here.

A Prayer for the Journey

Dear God,

Thank You for every lesson, every loss, and every moment that brought me closer to myself and to You.

Even when I didn't understand the plan, You were guiding me. Even in the hard, You were healing me.

Help me to carry these lessons forward with grace. Let my story be a source of strength—for myself and for others.

And as I continue on this journey, remind me: I am never walking alone.

Amen.

Reflection Prompt:

What lessons has your life taught you that continue to shape how you live, love, and lead?

Journaling Space

A Letter to the Woman You're Becoming

Before you grab a tissue (or a snack—because emotional breakthroughs call for snacks), let's keep it real. You've laughed, cried, scribbled in the margins, and maybe even yelled at a few pages. And yet—you're still here. Still growing. Still *becoming*. That's no small thing, sis.

You've shown up for every page, every prompt, every tear, and every truth. Now, it's time to bring it all together.

Write a letter to the woman you're becoming.

Tell her what you're proud of. What you've learned. What you're letting go of. And what you're stepping boldly into.

Speak to her like she's already here—because in so many ways, she is.

Let this be your final journal entry in this book—but the beginning of a beautiful new chapter in your life.

A Letter to the Woman You're Becoming:

Affirmation

I am no longer waiting for
permission to live fully.

I embody the wisdom I've gained, the lessons
I've learned, and the power I've reclaimed.

Every step I take is aligned with
the woman I'm becoming — bold,
worthy, and unstoppable.

I am the evidence of my own
transformation, and I rise without fear.

Epilogue
This Is Just the Beginning

You've made it to the final pages—but this isn't the end. Not by a long shot.

This book wasn't just meant to be read—it was meant to be *lived*. And the truth is, transformation is ongoing. Becoming is a lifelong journey, not a finish line.

There will still be hard days. Doubts may still whisper. But now, you have tools. You have truth. And most importantly—you have *you*.

Take everything you've learned, felt, and affirmed and walk boldly into the life that's been waiting on the real you to show up.

The woman you're becoming? She's not a future goal. She's a present truth.

So take the next step. Start the new chapter. Live as her.

And remember—you don't have to do it alone. This community, this sisterhood, this story—it walks with you.

With all my heart,

Tanya

About the Author

Tanya Stokes is a four-time bestselling author, poet, and creative visionary whose work empowers women to embrace authenticity, healing, and transformation. Through her raw storytelling and heartfelt honesty, she inspires readers to unlearn limitations, reclaim their worth, and rise into the fullness of who they are becoming.

Tanya is the founder of Compassionate Designs Publishing, where she guides emerging authors in sharing their voices with clarity and confidence. She is also the founder of the ANT777 Motorcycle Foundation, established in honor of her late son, which advocates for motorcycle safety and provides resources to riders and families.

Her previous works include My Muse, The Truth, Seasons Change, Echoes of Self and Soul, and the collaborative anthology Choose to Rise. Whether through books, art, or community work, Tanya's mission remains the same: to inspire growth, courage, and self-love in everyone she reaches.

www.ingramcontent.com/pod-product-compliance
Lightning Source LLC
Chambersburg PA
CBHW050246010526
44107CB00003B/202